NEW TERRITORY

NEW TERRITORY

CONTEMPORARY

INDIANA

FICTION

EDITED BY

Michael Wilkerson and Deborah Galyan

INDIANA UNIVERSITY PRESS   BLOOMINGTON & INDIANAPOLIS

Manufactured in the United States of America

Library of Congress Cataloging-in-Publication Data

New territory: contemporary Indiana fiction/edited by Michael Wilkerson and Deborah Galyan

p.   cm.

ISBN 0-253-36544-9 (alk. paper).—ISBN 0-253-20595-6 (pbk.: alk. paper)

1. American fiction—Indiana. 2. American fiction—20th century. 3. Indiana—Fiction. I. Wilkerson, Michael. II. Galyan, Deborah.

PS571.I6N49   1990

813'.010832772—dc20   90-30118

CIP

1 2 3 4 5 94 93 92 91 90

C O N T E N T S

INTRODUCTION

Michael Wilkerson and Deborah Galyan

One of the most challenging aspects of being a Hoosier writer is to discover and describe what makes Indiana unique. Though we may have beautiful scenery, we're not known for mountains, oceans, or sunshine; our economy and culture is so mixed that the name "Indiana" doesn't instantly connote anything like the wheat fields of Kansas, Minnesota's ten thousand lakes, or the famous potatoes of Idaho. The definition of our nickname is so unsettled, or perhaps unsatisfactory, that several years ago Dan Quayle delivered to the U.S. Senate his plea for a more positive dictionary portrayal of the term "Hoosier."

We had a more unified identity once. Ours was the largest bloc of the huge Northwest Territory before it was carved into states; later, Indiana became a key state in national politics, the farm economy, and American literature. But James Whitcomb Riley, Booth Tarkington, and Theodore Dreiser are now part of our past, and even postwar writers like Dan Wakefield and Kurt Vonnegut haven't lived here in more than thirty years.

Indiana continues to produce writers, and over the past decade they have begun to identify, imagine, and shape a new territory. Urbanization, the collapse of the family farm, and the expansion of mass media and culture have altered the Indiana landscape forever. The writers in this volume are exploring a literary landscape in which the mythological vision of a perpetually pastoral Indiana is acknowledged but often shattered. Some of the visions are uncomfortable, wacky, even paranoid, but each is unmistakably Hoosier.

Michael Martone's "Everybody Watching and the Time Passing Like That" is the tale of a contemporary Hoosier hero, James Dean, told by his high school drama teacher. She rescues Dean from the hands of Hollywood mythmakers and makes his story her own. Looking back through the lens of Dean's fame, Martone shows us a curiously talented and prophetic small-town Indiana boy, learning how to kiss and how to die.

Jesse Lee Kercheval's "A History of Indiana" portrays a small band of self-conscious and somewhat baffled pioneers attempting to impose their own mishmash of mythologies on the virgin territory of old Indiana; by the story's end, our origins are still little more than a blank slate, to be filled in further by other writers. Kercheval's was one of dozens of stories we received that still envisioned Indiana as a pioneer wilderness, even though the landscape has been settled, even urbanized, for generations.

Scott Russell Sanders uses the state as a springboard to world travel. In "The First Journey of Jason Moss," Sanders's Buddha, Indiana, protagonist finds a universe outside the small town and a Hoosierness within himself that translates across many cultures.

James Alexander Thom reconstructs a character's childhood memory of Indiana with exquisite sensual detail in "I Can If I May," an excerpt from his novel *Staying Out of Hell.* Thom's small town of ten-cent stores and vacant lots belongs to an earlier, seemingly innocent Indiana, but behind this simple frontispiece is a more ambiguous reality. Thom's young character lives in a place where the darkness of "unknowable things" such as racism, torture, and "meanness in the eyes of men" impinge upon a boy's fine, bright summer day.

In an excerpt from her novel *Lessons,* Lee Zacharias writes with acute perception of the contrast between the Bloomington university culture and the mill town that was Hammond in the early 1960s. Her character Jane Hurdle's bitter trip between those worlds in "The Night Coach to Bloomington" illustrates the profound economic and social barriers that exist between some intrastate regions.

In the 1980s, as in no other era in recent memory, the United States has been dominated by the culture of business. Ron Hansen's "Can I Just Sit Here for a While?" studies three youngish Indiana men who are creatures of that culture, their world view—and, it seems, an inner rage—confined and defined by their quest for material success.

Elizabeth Stuckey-French, writing "Blessing" in the present tense, portrays a family in quiet decline, occupying homeland that once was a huge native American settlement, that later typified the backbone of the state's family farm economy, that has now become a passive investment for a rich corporate chief.

Philosopher and writer William H. Gass focuses the ardor of his powerful language on a languishing pair of newlyweds, who seem to shrink in spirit as a bleak Lafayette winter traps them in their flimsy, undersized duplex. As the couple in "The First Winter of My Married Life" redefines itself in the terms of its confinement, the sustained bursts of Gass's descriptive fire riddle the dismal prospects of their failing marriage with dazzling energy.

Susan Neville re-energizes and re-connects us with a bona fide Hoosier mythic hero, Johnny Appleseed. Unlike his eighteenth-century forebear, Neville's modern-day Appleseed casts his magic beyond the Ohio River, all the way to Zanzibar.

Some of what is and has been happening in Indiana verges on the inexplicable and therefore must be transformed into myth. Brown County's Clarence Roberts, who was found dead twice in different arson-murders ten years apart, has become a contemporary Hoosier legend. His tale of misidentity becomes a symbol of our collective uncertainty about who we are in "The Clarence Roberts Mysteries."

We thought it fitting to end the book with David Moser's "Postcards," which seem to arrive from nowhere and to involve a random assortment of Bloomington residents in what may or may not be a coincidental series of calamitous encounters. Moser's piece suggests the death of an Indiana governed by church, family, and tradition; in his new Bloomington, community is a product of accident, chaos, or mathematical probability.

As a whole, these eleven stories depict an Indiana uprooted from family agriculture and small-town values. Elizabeth Stuckey-French's church is a place where holiness mingles with guilt and sin; the lawman in "The Clarence Roberts Mysteries" is the apparent source of corruption; and even basketball, worshipped in a modern palace by Ron Hansen's characters, cannot save them from their anger and loneliness.

None of the stories collected here can tell us exactly what will characterize the Indiana of the next century, but clearly, in literature as well as in life, we have begun to carve out a new territory.

This anthology is the product of well over a year's search for recent fiction about Indiana—through magazines, books, and other publications. We are indebted to the dozens of writers who sent us their works; to Jim Powell of the Indianapolis Writers' Center and Rob McPherson of the Indiana Arts Commission for helping us locate some of the stories in this volume; to Jean Kane for much good advice and assistance; and to John Gallman of Indiana University Press, whose idea this anthology originally was and whose high standards helped us make it a better volume. The ultimate test of any book, of course, is in the reading. We hope you enjoy *New Territory*.

Everybody Watching and the Time Passing Like That

Michael Martone

WHERE was I when I heard about it? Let's see. He died on that Friday, but I didn't hear until Saturday at a speech meet in Lafayette. I was in the cafetorium, drinking coffee and going over the notes I had made on a humorous interp I'd just finished judging. The results were due in a few minutes, and the cafetorium was filling up with students between rounds. I had drama to judge next and was wondering how my own kids had done in their first rounds. So, I was sitting there, flipping back and forth through the papers on my clipboard, drinking coffee, when Kevin Wilkerson came through the swinging doors. I saw him first through the windows in the doors, the windows that have the crisscrossing chicken wire sandwiched between the panes. He had this look on his face. I thought, "Oh my, I bet something's happened in his round." He looked like he'd done awful. But he'd probably flubbed a few words or dropped a line or two, or so I thought. I once judged a boy making his first speech who went up, forgot everything, and just stood there. Pretty soon there was a puddle on the floor and all of this in silence. The timekeeper sat there flipping over the cards. So I spoke up and repeated the last thing I could remember from his speech.

1

Something about harvesting the sea. And he picked up right there and finished every word, wet pants and all.

They were corduroy pants, I remember. He finished last in his round, but you've got to hand it to the boy. I'd like to say the same kid went on to do great things. But I can't because I never heard. So I tell this story to my own kids when they think they have done poorly, and I was getting ready to tell Kevin something like it as he came up to the table. Kevin was very good at extemp. He's a lawyer now, a good one, in Indianapolis. He said to me then, "Mrs. Nall, I'm afraid I've got some real bad news." And I must have said something like nothing could be as bad as the look on your face. Then he told me. "Jimmy Dean is dead. He died in a wreck."

They'd been listening to the car radio out in the parking lot between rounds. That's how they heard. "Are you all right, Mrs. Nall?" Kevin was saying. Now, I'm a drama teacher. I was Jimmy's first drama coach, as you know. I like to think I have a bit of poise, that I have things under control. I don't let myself in for surprises, you know. But when Kevin said that to me, I about lost it, my stage presence if you will, right there in the cafetorium. Then everyone seemed to know about it all at once, and all my students began showing up. They stood around watching to see what I'd do. Most of them had met Jimmy the spring before, you know, when he came home with the *Life* photographer. They just stood watching me there with the other students from the other schools kind of making room for us. Well, if I didn't feel just like that boy who'd wet his pants. Everybody watching and the time passing like that.

But you were wondering where I was, not how I felt.

I suppose, too, you'd like to know how I met James Dean, the plays we did in high school, the kids he hung around with and such. What magazine did you say you're from? I can tell you these things, though I don't quite understand why people like yourself come looking for me. I'm flattered—because I really didn't teach Jimmy to act. I have always said he was a natural that way. I think I see that something happened when he died. But something happens, I suppose, when anybody dies. Or is born for that matter.

I guess something is also gone when the last person who actually knew him dies. It's as if people come here to remember things that never happened to them. There are the movies, and the movies are good. It's just sometimes the people of Fairmount wonder what all the fuss is about. It isn't so much that the grave gets visited. You'd expect that. Why, every time you head up the pike to Marion, there is a strange car with out-of-state plates, bumping through the cemetery. It's just that then the visitors tend to spread out through town, knocking on doors.

Marcus and Ortense, his folks (well, not his parents, you know), say people still show up on the porch. They're there on the glider, sun up, when Ortense goes for the *Star.* Or someone will be taking pictures of the feedlot and ask to see Jimmy's bedroom. Why come to the home town? It's as if they were those students in the cafetorium just watching and waiting for things to happen after the news has been brought.

People are always going through Indiana. Maybe this is the place to stop. Maybe people miss the small town they never had.

I'm the schoolteacher, all right. I remember everyone. I have to stop myself from saying, "Are you Patty's little brother?" Or "The Wilton boy?"

That's small town.

The first I remember him, he was in junior high. I was judging a speech contest for the WCTU, and Jimmy was in it, a seventh grader. He recited a poem called "Bars." You see the double meaning there?

He started it up kneeling behind a chair, talking through the slats of the back, you know. Props. It wasn't allowed. No props. I stopped him and told him he would have to do it without the chair. But he said he couldn't do it that way. I asked him why not. He said he didn't know. He stood there on the stage. Didn't say one word. Well, just another boy gone deaf and dumb in front of me. One who knew the words.

I prompted him. He looked at the chair off to the side of the stage.

Couldn't speak without his little prison. So he walked off.

"Bars" was a monologue, you see. In high school, Jimmy did a monologue for me, for competition. "The Madman." We cut it from Dickens.

We took it to the Nationals in Colorado that year. Rode the train out there together for the National Forensic League tournament. As I said, it was a monologue. But it called for as many emotions as a regular interp which might have three or four characters. You never get more than five or six characters in a regular reading. But Jimmy had that many voices and moods in this single character. Could keep them straight. Could go back and forth with them. He was a natural actor. I didn't teach him that. Couldn't.

I know what you're thinking. You think that if you slice through a life anywhere you'll find the marbling that veins the whole cake. Not true. He was an actor. He was other people. Just because he could be mad doesn't mean he was.

You know the scene in the beanfield. Come to the window. There, you see that field? Beans.

They used mustard plants in the movie.

And here, we know that. Jimmy knew that too. Beans are bushier. Leave it to Hollywood to get it all wrong.

In the summer, kids here walk through the beans and hoe out the weeds. They wear white T-shirts and blue jeans in all that green. Jimmy walked too when he was here.

That's the town's favorite scene. Crops. Seeing that—those boys in the bushes, white shirts, blue pants. How could he have known how to be insane? Makes me want to seal off those fields forever. Keep out everything. You can understand that, can't you?

It was quiet then. Now the Air Guard jets fly over from Peru. I notice most people get used to it. At night, you can hear the trucks on I-69 right through your bed. I lost boys on that highway before it was even built. They'd go down to the Muncie exit and nudge around the barricades in their jalopies. Why, the road was still being built, you know. Machinery everywhere. Imagine that. How white that new cement must have been in the moonlight. Not a car on the road. This was before those yard lights the rural electric cooperative gives the farmers. Those boys would point their cars south to Indianapolis and turn out the lights, knowing it was supposed to be straight until Anderson. No signs. No stripes on the road. New road through the beanfields, through the cornfields. Every once and a while a smudge pot, a road lantern. That stretch of road was one of the first parts finished, and it sat there, closed for years it seemed, as the rest of the highway was built up to it along with the weight stations and the rest stops.

I think of those boys as lost on that road. In Indiana then, if you got killed on a marked road, the highway patrol put up a cross as a reminder to other drivers.

Some places looked just like a graveyard. But out on the unfinished highway, when those boys piled into a big yellow grader or a bulldozer blade or just kept going though the road stopped at a bridge that had yet to be built, it could be days before they were even found.

The last time I saw Jimmy alive, we were both driving cars. We did a little dance on Main Street. I was backing out of a parking slot in my Buick Special when Jimmy flashed by in the Winslows' car. I saw him in the rearview mirror and craned my neck around. At the same time, I laid on the horn.

One long blast.

Riding with Jimmy was that *Life* photographer who was taking pictures of everything.

Jimmy had on his glasses, and his cap was back on his head.

He slammed on the brakes and threw his car in reverse, backing up the street, back past me. He must have recognized my car. So out I backed, out across the front of his car, broadsiding his grille, then to the far outside lane where I lined up parallel with him.

He was a handsome boy. He already had his window rolled down, saying something, and I was stretching across the front seat, trying to reach the crank to roll down mine on the passenger side. Flustered, I hadn't thought to put the car in park. So I had to keep my foot on the brake. My skirt rode up my leg, and I kept reaching and then backing off to get up on one elbow to take a look out the window to see if Jimmy was saying something.

The engine was running fast, and the photographer was taking pictures.

I kept reaching for the handle and feeling foolish that I couldn't reach it. I was embarrassed. I couldn't think of any way to do it. You know how it is—you're so busy doing two things foolishly, you can't see through to doing one thing at a time. There were other cars getting lined up behind us, and they were blowing their horns. Once in history, Fairmount had a traffic jam.

The fools. They couldn't see what was going on.

Jimmy started pointing up ahead and nodding, and he rolled up his window and took off. I scrunched back over to the driver's side as Jimmy roared by. He honked his horn, you know. *A shave and a haircut.* The cars that had been stacked up behind us began to pass me on the right, I answered back. *Two bits.*

I could see that photographer leaning back over the bench seat, taking my picture. I flooded the engine. I could smell the gasoline. I sat there on Main Street getting smaller.

When the magazine with the pictures of Jimmy and Fairmount came out, we all knew it would be worth saving, that sometime in the future it would be a thing to have. Some folks went all the way up to Fort Wayne for copies. But Jimmy was dead, so it was sold out up there too.

I wasn't in the magazine. No picture of me in my car on Main Street. But there was Jimmy walking on Washington with the Citizen's Bank onion dome over his shoulder. Jimmy playing a bongo to the livestock. Jimmy reading James Whitcomb Riley. Jimmy posing with his cap held on his curled arm. He wears those rubber boots with the claw buckles. His hand rests on the boar's back.

Do you remember that one beautiful picture of Jimmy and the farm? He's in front of the farm, the white barn and the stone fences in the background. The trees are just beginning to bud. Tuck, Jimmy's dog, is looking one way and Jimmy the other. There is the picture, too, of Jimmy sitting upright in the coffin.

Mr. Hunt of Hunt's Store down on Main Street kept a few coffins around.

That is where that picture was taken.

In Indianapolis, they make more coffins than anywhere else in the world. The trucks, loaded up, go through town every day. They've got CASKETS painted in red on the sides of the trailers.

You wait long enough downtown, one'll go through.

See what you have made me do? I keep remembering the wrong things. I swear, you must think that's all I think about.

What magazine did you say you were from?

Jim's death is no mystery to me. It was an accident. An accident. There is no way you can make me believe he wanted to die. I'm a judge. I judge interpretations. There was no reason. Look around you, look around. Those fields. Who could want to die? Sure, students in those days read EC comics. I had a whole drawer full of them. I would take them away for the term. Heads axed open. Limbs severed. Skin being stripped off. But I was convinced it was theater. Look, they were saying, we can make you sick.

It worked. They were right.

I'd look at those comic books after school. I'd sit at my desk and look at them. Outside the window, the hall monitors would be cleaning out the board erasers by banging them against the wall of the school. The air out there was full of chalk. I flipped through those magazines, nodding my head, knowing what it was all about. I am not a speech teacher for nothing. I taught acting. I know when someone wants attention. The thing is to make them feel things before anything else.

I taught Jimmy to kiss.

I taught Jimmy to die.

We were doing scenes from *Of Mice and Men*. I told him the dying part is pretty easy. The gun George uses is three inches from the back of Lenny's head. When it goes off, your body will go like this—the shoulders up around the ears, the eyes pressed closed. He was on his knees saying something like "I can see it, George." Then *bang*. Don't turn when you fall. After your body flinches, relax. Relax every muscle. Your body will fall forward all by itself.

Well, it didn't, not with Jimmy. He wanted to grab his chest like some kid playing war. Or throw up his hands. Or be blown forward from the force of the shot.

"Haven't you ever seen anything die?" I asked him.

"No," he said.

"It's like this," I said, and I got up there on the stage and fell over again and again. I had George shoot me until we ran out of blanks. It was October, I remember, and outside the hunters were walking the fields flushing pheasants. After we were done with the practice, we could hear the popping of shotguns—one two, one two. We hadn't noticed that with our own gun fire.

Hunting goes so fast and that's what irritates me.

Jimmy was so excited, you know, doing things you couldn't do in high school. Dying, kissing. That's how young they were. Kids just don't know that acting is doing things that go on every day.

"Just kiss," I told Jimmy after he'd almost bent a girl's neck off. "Look," I said, taking one of his hands and putting it on my hip, "close your eyes." I slid my hands up under his arms so that my hands pressed his shoulder blades. His other hand came around. He stood there, you know. I tucked my head to the side and kissed him.

"Like that," I said.

I quieted the giggles with a look. And then I kissed him again.

"Do it like that," I said.

Even pretending, Jimmy liked things real. No stories, action. He was doing a scene once, I forget just what. The set for the scene called for a wall with a bullet hole. Jimmy worked on the sets too. I was going to paint the hole on the wall, and Jimmy said no. We waited as he rushed home. He came back with a .22, and before I could stop him, he shot a hole in the plywood wall.

I tell you, the hole was more real than that wall. I remember he went up to the wall and felt it, felt the hole.

"Through and through," he said. "Clean through and through."

The bullet had gone through two curtains and lodged in the rear wall of the stage. I can show you that hole. If you want to look, I can show you.

Right before he died, Jimmy made a commercial for the Highway Safety Council. They show it here twice a year in the driver's education class. The day they show it, I sit in. The students in the class each have a simulator. You know, a steering wheel, a mirror, a windshield with wipers that work, dials luminous in the dark.

Jimmy did the commercial while he was doing his last picture. He is dressed up as a cowboy, twirling a lariat. Gig Young interviews him. They talk about racing and going fast. Then Gig Young asks Jimmy, the cowboy, for advice. Advice for all the young drivers who might be watching. And I look around the class, and they are watching.

It is the way he begins each sentence with "Oh."

Or it's the lariat, the knot he fiddles with.

That new way of acting.

What is he thinking about? Jimmy was supposed to say the campaign slogan—*The life you save may be your own.* But he doesn't. He looks toward the camera. He couldn't see the camera because he wouldn't wear his glasses. I can see what is happening. He is forgetting. He says, "The life you save may be"—a pause—"mine." Mine.

I guess that I have seen that little bit of film more times than anyone else in the world. I watch the film, and he talks to me, talks to me directly. I have it all up here.

He kissed me.

He died.

Leave his life alone.

I know motivation. I *teach* motivation. I teach *acting*.

A History of Indiana

Jesse Lee Kercheval

ALL HIS life, Lancelot Walker would remember the plague of squirrels.

At that time New Hope had existed for just thirteen months. The whole first year no one knew anything, and that was painful. No one knew when to trust the thawed earth enough to plant. No one knew when the frost would come again. That year there were three families and Walker, their bachelor. Even so they couldn't agree on anything. Walker wanted to name the settlement Camelot. He didn't see any harm in it.

"Camelot, Mother of Harlots," declared Mrs. McLintock, the matriarch of the two Georgia families. Mr. Bingham, who was English, thought it smacked of monarchy. "Too much history," he said, "it doesn't seem American."

So New Hope it was, though Walker thought it a melancholy choice. It implied a trail of blasted hopes behind them, and even if that was true, he didn't see why they had to make it official.

That first spring they couldn't even agree what to plant. Walker and the two Georgia families were for corn, but Bingham wanted to plant wheat and hedge with potatoes. "Well, think of Rome," Walker said, trying to lend a little perspective to their troubles. "Do you think Romulus and Remus knew right off what to do?" It seemed to Walker they probably had less to go on, if they were raised by wolves.

"I suppose you think they planted corn," Mr. Bingham said.

"Well, I'm sure as hell they didn't plant potatoes," Walker said.

"Rome," Mrs. McLintock said, "is the Seven-Headed Beast that was and is not but will be."

They planted. The corn and wheat grew. The potatoes rotted.

Walker spent the first January snowed in his cabin, making up a list of names for plants people had spent the summer calling things like *pricky bush* and *big bud*. He went through Livy and Mallory—*Brutus Blade, Cleopatra's Tears, Excaliber Leaf*. He didn't mean to lose the next time.

By the second March things began to repeat themselves, and life seemed on the edge of predictability. The snow melted on time. The ground warmed up, and everyone planned on planting both corn and wheat. Three Welsh families came straggling over the creek and cleared land. That doubled the population, and the whole of New Hope had Mrs. Bingham's second annual piano concert to look forward to. None of the new families had been at the first concert, of course, but they realized what it meant on the frontier to take part in a second annual anything.

It was at the second annual concert that Lancelot Walker met Gwen Llewellyn for the first time.

"Guinevere," Walker said, taking her hand.

"She's just a plain Gwen, Mr. Walker," her father corrected as his daughter became the first person in New Hope to have her hand kissed in greeting. But Gwen had never heard of Arthur's queen and didn't know she was in danger of history. She paid more attention to the piano, which rose from clawed feet to a music stand carved into two griffins—rampant. She had never seen one before.

Walker was sorry she wasn't looking at him but respected her for her love of music. The first concert had been his doing. He was at the Binghams' one morning arguing corn versus wheat and staring at the only musical instrument in New Hope when something rose up in him. He pushed past Bingham and into the kitchen where Mrs. Bingham was boiling porridge.

"Spring awaits you, Persephone. Rise up and play for us!" he cried out to her.

Mrs. Bingham put her spoon down, wiped her hands on her apron. "All right, Mr. Walker," she said. "Since you put it that way."

Mr. Bingham had to put up with cold porridge while his wife rehearsed, but now, in the second year, he was inclined to see it as a sacrifice for the greater good.

"Karl Ditters Von Dittersdorf," Mrs. Bingham said and seated herself at the piano in a thunderstorm of purple silk.

"Alas, that once great city," Mrs. McLintock whispered to her daughter, "that was clothed in purple."

The music started.

Gwen's father always said of his daughter, "That one's closed tight as a fist." But at the instant Mrs. Bingham struck the first chord, Gwen looked at Walker and caught him looking at her. She took the music as a gift from him. He smiled, and she smiled back.

When Mrs. Bingham had played every note she knew, repeated exactly the previous year's performance, the concert was over. New Hope clapped and rose, stretching. It was then that Walker heard a sound like something hitting the roof.

"Is that hail?" someone asked. Mr. Bingham opened the door.

The fence, the yard, every tree and stump was covered with squirrels. Walker went out. Squirrels were running across the roof, and did sound like hail. They chased each other in circles in the yard like leaves might in a storm. But mostly they looked and sounded like squirrels, hundreds and hundreds of squirrels. Squirrels chewing on the rails and shingles and the bark of the trees. Squirrels as far as anyone could see.

"The wheat!" Mr. Bingham ran by with an ax. When the first dead squirrel came flying out of his grain bin, they all broke and ran—"The corn cribs!" There was much nailing of boards across cracks before each family went to bed under its own roof of squirrels.

The squirrels were still there in the morning. Still there the next day. They ate the swelling buds off the trees. Walker couldn't get over how strange it was no one had seen the squirrels' arrival. "Where do you think they came from?" he asked Bingham.

"Better to ask where we should go," he said, and everyone shook their heads. There was no point in planting corn or wheat if the squirrels would eat it as soon as it came up, and, if they waited much longer, it would be too late to clear land and plant somewhere else—in New New Hope.

"The Lord Jehovah smote the Philistines," Mrs. McLintock said, "with a plague of hemorrhoids."

The next day it rained, but the wet squirrels still sat and chewed. Everyone's roof leaked.

"What we need is some information," Walker said as they all sat in front of the McLintock fireplace. "I mean how often do the squirrels come? Not every year—we know that. But every other year? Every hundred years?"

"How about how long they stay?" Mr. Llewellyn put in.

"Or how to kill them?" said Mrs. McLintock.

"More like, should we head north or west?" said Bingham.

Walker stood up. "Indians," he said, "are the ones who'd know."

"There aren't any Indians here," Bingham said, and, for the first time, this seemed a bad omen not a good one. What if the Indians knew better? Or had all starved?

"In Lewis and Clark's journal," Walker said, "there's report of a tribe of Indians on the Ohio descended from a Welsh prince named Madoc. I met a trader on the way out here who'd heard about them and said damned if he didn't have half a mind to go see."

"White Indians?" Bingham said. "Welsh Indians?"

Llewellyn shrugged—he'd gotten here.

"I'm going east to find out about these squirrels," Walker said. Everyone looked east. "But I need someone who speaks Welsh." Llewellyn stopped looking east.

"I'll go," Gwen said.

"A woman might be less threatening," Bingham agreed.

Walker shook Llewellyn's hand. "Think of your daughter," he said, "as the Joan of Arc of New Hope."

They left the next morning. The first day every tree they passed was top to bottom with squirrels. The second day they could still hear squirrels moving from branch to branch. But the third day the forest was quiet and empty. The fourth day they came to the Ohio. They went upstream until they found a ford and waded across. On the other side, they sat and put their boots on. The bank was steep and seemed to have been reinforced with cut logs. Smoke rose from a fire they couldn't see. After a while, a woman came to the top of the bank and threw off some trash.

"Hey!" Walker said. The woman shrugged. They sat a while longer, and four men appeared and began to pick their way down to the river. One sat on a boulder about twenty feet off, and three came on. Then another sat down, and another, until finally the oldest man sat down so close his knees touched Gwen's. The Chief had straight dark hair a little longer than Gwen's. Walker thought he saw a resemblance.

"Okay," Walker said, nodding to Gwen.

" 'r wiwerod," Gwen said, wrinkling her face and bringing her hands up like paws. Walker heard one more distinct *wiwerod* and then the Welsh really started to fly. Gwen kept up the pantomime as well, adding a bushy tail to her squirrel. She held out an open hand, let one finger rise from it like growing corn—before her other-hand-as-squirrel nibbled the finger back down to the ground. Gwen's sentences started to go up at the end, and Walker guessed she'd gotten past facts into questions. She pointed east. She pointed west. She shrugged. The Chief started to talk. He pointed at them. He pointed at himself. He tapped his nose twice. The Chief's face was blank—but then he was an Indian. Gwen's face was too, but no more than usual.

"Well?" Walker said.

"I can't understand him," she said, "and I don't think he understands me either." They all looked at each other. Then the Chief turned around and yelled to the man behind him, who passed it on, and another man came down from the invisible village—the trader Walker had met.

"How the hell are you?" the trader asked, sitting down next to the Chief.

Walker told him about the squirrels.

"Well, damn," he said.

"He doesn't seem," Walker said, nodding toward the Chief, "to speak Welsh."

"Well, Goddamn."

"How do you talk to them?"

"I parlay French—all the Indians on the Ohio speak a little of that. You want I should talk to him?"

"Please."

"Les ecureuils," the trader started, wrinkling his face at the Chief in his own squirrel imitation. The trader turned back to Walker. "What do you want to ask?"

"Where the squirrels came from and how we can get them to go back there."

The trader asked.

The Chief answered.

"Well, damn," the trader said. "He says that you're asking the wrong questions."

"Damn yourself," Walker said.

"Ask him," Gwen said, "to tell us what he knows about the squirrels."

The Chief swam his hand through the air as he answered.

"He says," the trader translated, "that they're fish." The Chief drew a wavy line in the dirt with his finger. "And fish swim in a river."

"What's that supposed to mean?" said Walker.

"Well," said the trader, "sometimes I don't understand them myself. It could be I'm getting all the words but not what they mean—I mean, would the Chief here get what I meant if I told him I was washed in the blood of the Lamb? But then again," the trader shrugged, "he could be just jerking you around."

The Chief stood up. He took Gwen by the shoulders and kissed her firmly on each cheek—as if she were Joan of Arc. Then he left, his men following.

"Well, Hell," the trader said, leaving too. "Don't do anything I wouldn't do."

They recrossed the river. "Fish," Walker said.

"Fish," he said again when they stopped for the night, and put his head in his hands. "Fi . . ." he started, but Gwen stopped him. "Don't say it," she said and, taking off her dress, made a gift of herself.

"Can I talk to your father?" Walker said to her later. "You do know I want to marry you, don't you?"

Gwen rolled over. "You're asking the wrong questions again."

In the morning they began to see squirrels passing in groups overhead. The next day the trees were full of them. One squirrel to a square foot of bark, Walker figured.

"Swim," Gwen yelled at them, flapping her arms. Two panicked squirrels ran forward and fought for a place on the next tree, their places in the rear taken in an instant.

Walker kicked a tree, "Swim." A half-dozen squirrels ran forward, and a half-dozen behind them moved up. "Sshh," he said, and they stood quiet. Even without prompting, every few minutes some squirrels changed trees—always moving forward—toward New Hope.

"Stay here," Walker said, and went off the path. After about fifty feet, the squirrels thinned out; after sixty, the trees were empty. He came back.

"They're going somewhere," he said.

"To New Hope."

"Maybe."

When they reached New Hope, there was no smoke coming from the Llewellyns'. Standing outside Walker could tell the place was empty, but Gwen went in anyway, closing the door behind her. The other chimneys were still smoking so Walker knew everyone hadn't cleared out yet. He went through New Hope to the woods on the other side. The trees were full of squirrels—still moving west.

When he got to his cabin, he saw Gwen out planting his corn. She straightened up and handed him the sack. By the time New Hope realized they were back, he had a half-sack of seed corn in the ground.

They all stood dumb watching him plant. The squirrels watching too. "What's this?" Bingham asked when Walker got to the end of the field.

Walker put down the sack of corn. "These squirrels are headed somewhere, and I intend to follow them until I find out. But first I'm going to get in my early corn."

"A time to plant," Mrs. McLintock said. She nodded at the squirrels, "and a time to pluck."

Walker put in another half-sack—as if an extra ten pounds would hold New Hope until he got back. It was almost dark when he left his cabin.

"Da left the family Bible for me," Gwen said. She held a large book against her chest.

Walker took her arm, which was as thin and hard as a tree branch. "He knew you might need it," he said.

"Go on," she said, shaking her head, shaking her arm free. Walker started toward the woods. Looking back, he saw her standing with the book open in front of her, though it was too dark to read. "That which is far off," she called, "and exceedingly deep, who can find it out?"

They all sat watching Walker's field. They were in agreement now. If the first shoot came up and got eaten, they would leave. The day after Walker left, three trappers drifted in and started banging away at the squirrels.

"How much do you get for a squirrel fur?" Bingham asked them when they'd made a big pile in the middle of town.

"Nothing," one of them said, and spit. "We're gonna jerk 'em." Which Mrs. Bingham explained to her husband meant dry the meat for winter. But when the trappers slit the squirrels, their knives hit bone right under the skin. There was no meat on them, and their stomachs were full of splinters. The trappers shot a few more, out of habit, then gave it up and sat with everyone else watching Walker's invisible corn.

After six days, there was still no sign of Walker or his corn. The grass on the edge of the field was starting to sprout and each blade seemed to come up under a squirrel. Mrs. McLintock shook her head. "I have lived an alien in a strange land," she said.

"So we have," Bingham said.

"Me and mine will be leaving," Mrs. McLintock said, "at sunup." Then Bingham thought Walker had been right about the town's name—How sad to leave New Hope behind with old. The trappers spent the day digging lead shot out of the dead squirrels. Then two of them headed west. Maybe they'd run into Walker or find out what had become of him and maybe not. At any rate west was the direction they always went—west and further west.

"Head north," the trapper who stayed behind advised Mrs. McLintock, while whispering in her daughter's ear, "Come west." Everyone except Gwen spent the night packing. But the Llewellyns hadn't left Gwen anything that needed packing, so no one could tell if she was going to leave or stay.

It was the quiet that woke everyone up. When Bingham opened his door and saw no squirrels, it was almost as much of a shock as seeing the squirrels the first time. The roof was empty, the fences, the trees. An hour later, Walker came home. He went right to his field, stood looking at it until everyone in New Hope was there. Then he told them what had happened. It was a story he only told once, but everyone remembered it. Years later a New Hoper working for the Indianapolis *Free Democrat Locomotive* would write his own version and put the story into history.

> The reports that come to us recently from Chicago of the sightings of strange airships should not be taken by the public as a thing altogether without precedence. A certain respected citizen of New Hope—well known in the state as a honest, non-drinking man—thirty years ago saw such a sight right here in Indiana. "The vessel was thirty feet in length," he reported, "and shaped like a bread pan with a loaf risen in it—all the color of new tin. Near the vessel was the most beautiful being I ever beheld. She was rather over-size, but of the most exquisite form and with eyes of sapphire and features such as would put shame to the statues of the ancient Greeks. She was dressed in nature's garb and her golden hair, wavy and glossy, hung to her waist, unconfined excepting by a band of glistening jewels that bound it back from her forehead. The jewels threw out rays of light as she moved her head. She was plucking little flowers that were just blossoming from the sod with exclamations of delight in a language I could not understand. Her voice was like low, silvery bells, and her laughter rang out like chimes. In one hand she carried a fan of curious design that she fanned herself vigorously with, though to me the air was not warm, and I wore an overcoat. On the far side of the vessel stood a man of lesser proportions, though of majestic countenance. He also was fanning himself with a curious fan as if the heat oppressed him.
>
> "Was this," I wondered, "Adam and Eve come to earth again?"

The newspaper reporter didn't mention the squirrels, years later maybe they didn't seem important. But squirrels there certainly were as Walker made his way west. He had to tie his hat on to protect himself from squirrels who, missing a particularly inspired forward leap, fell to the ground like two-pound hail. On the second day he began to hear a sound, a single high note that seemed to shift from one ear to the other. He shook his head. The squirrels around him shook theirs. The third day he came out of the woods on the edge of a large clearing. The squirrels were so thick on the ground that he couldn't move without stepping on them. Walker was afraid they might panic suddenly when he got into the clearing. A thousand squirrels would run up the tallest thing in sight—him. So he cut a branch and moved forward, sweeping a dozen squirrels aside for each step. In the middle of the clearing was the bread pan. And the naked woman. The high-pitched noise was coming from the ship. But the woman opened her mouth and made a sound that wasn't too different from the one the ship was making. It made his ears itch. Walker, thinking about the Welsh Indians, almost lost heart for the whole business. But he went forward, starting Gwen's squirrel imitation. It helped that there were a thousand thousand squirrels in a circle around him to point to by way of example. He pointed east. He did the finger-as-corn eaten by hand-as-squirrel. He rubbed his stomach, sucked in his cheeks—tried generally to look faced with starvation.

It was then he saw the man. The woman said something, and the man came around from the other side of the ship, making marks on a piece of flat tin. *Nine hundred thousand and one, nine hundred thousand and two . . .* He's counting the squirrels, Walker realized, watching each mark. The woman finished talking to the man and turned back to Walker. She pointed to her ship. She held up three fingers.

"Three what?" Walker asked.

She pointed at the sun, then moved her arm three times in an arc across the sky, her breasts making their own gentle revolutions.

"Three days," Walker said, holding up three of his own fingers in acknowledgment. The woman nodded. The man moved away, marking on his tin again. The woman watched him for a moment, then shook her head, and something in the way she did it made Walker think, "She's his mother."

The woman looked back at Walker and smiled. She took him by the wrist—her hand was hot. She pointed at him, touched her own chest, pointed at the ship, pointed up. Walker threw his head back and looked at the sky, blue and endless overhead. He felt he was at the bottom of a deep clear well. His lungs ached. He wanted to swim up, burst into what was beyond, into air he had been waiting all his life to breathe. The woman was looking up too. Her fingers burned on his wrist. Against the blue of the sky, her face was white as milk— inhuman. Walker wondered if he knew her name and spoke it, would she disappear with a puff of smoke and a scream like Morgan le Fay? She looked down, and her face was flushed. She looked lonely. Walker shook his head. He took her hand from his wrist and touched it to his lips. It was like kissing a stove. She blushed—red spreading from the roots of her hair to her breasts and maybe lower, though Walker didn't look.

He could feel her watching him as he swept his way out of the clearing. The squirrels stood on their hind legs, and it struck Walker that they looked like little humans wearing fur suits. When he looked back from the edge of the woods, the afternoon sun gave them fur halos. For three days the trees he passed were more full of squirrels than ever. The third night he slept as trees groaned with squirrels. He woke up to absolute quiet.

"They're really gone then," Bingham said.

Walker nodded.

"They was angels," Mrs. McLintock said. "Unfallen creations of God like Adam and Eve, walking naked and not ashamed."

"Well," Walker said, "maybe."

"And they're in Heaven now," she said. "Oh, behold! I heard the voice of many angels round about the throne and the beasts and the elders: and the number of them was ten thousand times ten thousand, and thousands of thousands."

"Angels," Bingham asked, "or squirrels?"

"But why," Mrs. Bingham asked, "didn't you go with her?"

"Because Gwen's agreed to marry me," Walker said. Gwen shook her head, but let Walker take her hand.

"Because you had corn in the ground, you mean," Bingham said.

Mrs. Bingham sighed, as if she saw years of cooked porridge and concerts clearly before her.

Then Walker heard a scratching sound. Everyone else heard it too. On a tree beside his cabin was a squirrel. There was no mistaking that. But it was completely white—an albino. The trapper drew a bead on it with his rifle, eased his finger onto the trigger.

"Don't," Walker said, and knocked the barrel up. The ball went whirring through the high branches. The squirrel didn't flinch. "It's deaf." He stood at the base of the tree. "Swim!" he yelled, "Get!" The squirrel looked like a white X painted on the tree. It hadn't heard its other-worldly summons.

"His head and his hairs were white like wool," Mrs. McLintock cried out, "as white as snow! And his feet like unto fine brass, as if they burned in a furnace! And out of his mouth went a sharp two-edged sword! And when I saw him—I FELL DOWN AT HIS FEET AS DEAD!" She went over like a tree. "Thank-you, Jesus!" she said as her sons carried her inside.

Everyone went home to plant.

Gwen put her arm through Walker's. "You should have let him shoot that squirrel," she said. "It won't bring you luck." Walker shook his head.

The squirrel looked down at him with eyes as blue and empty as the sky.

The First Journey of Jason Moss

Scott Russell Sanders

ONE DAY in October an accountant from Buddha, Indiana, decided the time had come for him to set out on a journey around the earth. Although Jason Moss had always felt a terrible passion for women, as a man might have a passion for billiards or pies, a deep shyness had kept him a bachelor, and so he had no need of explaining his journey to any wife or child. No goodbyes were needed for his kinfolk either. They all lived elsewhere, mostly in trailers on the coasts of Oregon and Maine, where they hunted mushrooms and carved figurines out of tree roots. Every Christmas they would write to him—Box 12, Buddha, Indiana—and send him photographs of a woodstove they had built from an oil drum, or a packet of seeds for growing foot-long cucumbers, or a newspaper clipping about the extinction of Siberian weasels. He would answer these letters promptly, saying that business was good, the weather bad, and his life ticking on as usual.

And so things had kept ticking along until his forty-seventh birthday, which fell in the middle of apple season. To mark the day, Jason always drove out to Burley's Orchard, where he picked two bushels of Winesaps, enough to keep him in fruit until spring brought rhubarb. On this particular birthday, after his baskets were full, he was standing tiptoe on the highest rung and reaching for one final apple when the ladder slipped. During the split second of his fall, he remembered the last glimpse of his father waving from the door of a boxcar, remembered helping his mother drag home a tombstone from an auction, and he realized that he was utterly sick of adding up columns of numbers, sick of hearing doors slam in his rooming house, sick of living womanless in Buddha, and he vowed that if he survived the landing he would set out on a trip and not stop until he had circled the planet.

Jason hit the ground without breaking a bone.

That night he took down his catalogs of backpacking gear. Since he had been poring over the various editions of these catalogs for years, he already knew which items to order. As many things as possible should be green, because that struck him as the proper color for traveling: a green rucksack and sleeping bag, green tent, green shirts and trousers and waterproof jacket, a slouch hat of green felt and green nylon laces for his boots. Along with the order for boots he enclosed a sheet of paper on which he had carefully outlined his stockinged foot.

Packages arrived for him all winter.

"Setting up a store?" the mailman asked.

"Just some things I've been needing," Jason replied.

When all the gear had been delivered he practiced stuffing it into the rucksack. The loaded pack weighed forty pounds, about one-quarter as much as Jason himself. Dressed in green and propped on the walking-stick, which blossomed into an umbrella at the flick of a button, he shouldered the rucksack and posed before the bathroom mirror. Hardly an imposing figure, he conceded. Skinny, bespectacled, a clerical sag in the spine. No one could mistake him for a voyageur. But he had never much cared what other people thought of him.

All winter he studied maps, planning his route. Wherever there was land he would simply walk, or perhaps hitch rides, and when he reached the edge of a continent he would sail. About the walking he felt no qualms, because for years it had been his habit to amble on weekends through the woods near town. His legs were bony, perhaps, and bowed, yet quite sound. Sailing might present more of a challenge, for Jason had never seen an ocean and had never set foot in any craft larger than the canoes he paddled on Syrup Creek. He had visited Lake Michigan, which was too wide to see across, and had watched cargo ships docking in Chicago, but such experience would hardly prepare him for crossing the sea. Prepared or not, he felt certain he would find a way, once he set out, to keep going.

Of course he could not set out immediately, not even when the last of the hiking equipment arrived with the warm weather in April. First he had to inform his clients that he would no longer be able to keep track of their money. Breaking the news to his landlady, who hated changes, took a week.

"That's a cockamamie idea if I ever heard one," she railed at him. But eventually she grew reconciled to the scheme, and advised him to rub alcohol on the soles of his feet, which would toughen them, and always to wear wool socks.

There were forms to fill out at the insurance company and post office. His savings, which after decades of shrewd living were substantial, had to be invested in such a way that even five years from now, even in Tasmania, he would be able to pay for whatever he needed. Delivering his clothes to the Salvation Army kept him busy for an afternoon. He had to find homes for thirty-four houseplants, including some finicky African violets and a rambunctious aloe that had won a red ribbon at the county fair.

Having at last cut himself free of people and having reduced his possessions to what could be carried in the rucksack, he still had to decide in which direction to begin his trip, whether east or west. If he nosed west into the prevailing winds, he could be guided by the sounds and smells of things. In Illinois he might be able to sniff the pigs of Iowa. In Utah he might hear the humming of rain on the ridges of the Sierras. Ever since Marco Polo revealed how long and toilsome were the eastern routes, all the great explorers had journeyed westward, Hudson and de La Salle and Daniel Boone, Lewis and Clark, the men whose travels Jason had studied since childhood. But if he set out eastward, he would not have to squint into the afternoon sun. Most days the wind would be at his back, helping him along, and his steps would be aligned with the spinning of the earth.

In the end he chose sunrise over sunset and headed east. He was accompanied to the edge of town by his Vietnamese laundress, his Argentine barber, several former clients asking final questions about their money, a boy whom he had once helped with algebra, and by the landlady, who presented him with a handsome pair of green wool socks.

"Remember," she said, "there's always a home for you in Buddha. And rub your feet with alcohol."

Jason hoisted the walking stick to wave back at them. Then he faced Ohio and took his first true step.

Each of these steps was, on average, thirty inches long, which meant 2,112 paces to the mile. At three miles per hour, eight hours a day, every week he would take 354,816 steps and cover 168 miles. In just under three weeks he would lift each boot a million times. If he maintained the same pace on the oceans as on land, he would circle the earth in a thousand days. The land portion of this circumambulation would require 16,727,040 steps, assuming he walked the whole way.

With these numbers buzzing around his head, Jason made his way down the Cincinnati highway. His calculations were soon in need of revising, however, for within an hour he accepted a ride in a chicken truck. On its side was painted BUDDHA'S BETTER BROILERS. The chickens were so crammed in their cages that a deaf person seeing the truck from a distance might have thought it was loaded with snow. A person with good working ears could have made no mistake.

Jason heaved his rucksack onto the seat and climbed in beside it. The driver was a bear-shaped woman with skin the color of wheat bread and eyes that made him think of pirates.

"Where you headed, bowlegs?" she roared above the noise of the chickens.

"Around the world," Jason shouted back.

"Lucky dog. Wish I was. But I've got to come on home after dumping these squawkers in Cincy. Listen to them. You ever hear such a racket? It's all I hear seven blessed days a week. Hens! Nearest thing an animal can get to pure dumb without expiring. Shoot, if I didn't have the four kids I'd buy me a backpack and go with you." She glared across at him. "Say, you married?"

Jason admitted that he was a bachelor. The woman's presence filled the cab like the smell of fresh biscuits, and filled him with yearning. Could he stand to meet and leave a woman each day for a thousand days?

"That's pure waste, if you ask me," she said, "a healthy galoot like you and no wife. There's not enough men to go around as it is, when you get up in the neighborhood of fifty. They die off right and left. My old man walked under a concrete chute, arguing with the foreman about a baseball game, and that put out his lights. Made himself into a statue."

"I'm sorry to hear that," said Jason.

"He wasn't much account. Warm in bed, though, and a set of ears at the dinner table." Without warning, she slammed her fist against the cab's rear window, yelling, "Stupid birds!" Jason leapt, but the chickens never hushed. Then she added gruffly, "Travel the world, you ought to find a sweetie somewhere."

"One never knows," he answered.

"Hey, listen, do me a favor. They say the Japanese have bred up this mute chicken that lays three eggs a day. Would you check that out for me?"

"I'll certainly inquire," said Jason. He scribbled the query into his pocket notebook. "And to whom should I address my reply?"

"Doris Wilkins. Rural Route 3, Buddha."

Be bold, he thought, and asked her, "Why haven't I ever seen you in town? I'm an accountant, and I thought I knew all the business people."

"My farm's four miles out. I only go into the burg for groceries. What few bucks I make I can add in my head."

"Do you raise the chickens yourself?"

"With my own little hands." She lifted both meaty fists from the steering wheel by way of illustration.

"I've never met a chicken grower before."

"And I never met an accountant. So we're even."

"I suppose somebody has to raise them," Jason observed.

"They don't just wander into the supermarket from the woods." With her hands once again on the wheel, she turned those piratical eyes on him. "Before you get through traveling, you're going to meet a lot of things you never bumped into before."

On a wharf in Cincinnati, Doris Wilkins gave him a crushing bearhug and introduced him to a barge captain who was bound for Pittsburgh with a load of coal. "Give this guy a lift," she told the captain. "He's going around the world."

Driving away, the chicken truck left a swirl of white feathers in its wake. Jason watched the spiraling fluff a long while after the truck had disappeared.

The captain could answer none of his questions about sailing, but he was an expert at stamp collecting. All the way up the Ohio River, while Jason gazed out the window counting smokestacks and dumps and huddles of trees along the banks, the captain talked about first-day covers, plate blocks, cachets, mint-sheets. Hauling album after album down from a shelf and spreading them across Jason's knees, the captain showed him stamps triangular and hexagonal, stamps depicting butterflies and biplanes and dead dictators, stamps in a rainbow of shades.

"This one here," the captain said, fingering a thick album, "has got an uncanceled stamp in it from every country in the U.N. except Upper Volta. You wouldn't be going through Upper Volta, would you?"

"I just might," said Jason, writing the name of the place in his notebook. "If I do, I'll be sure to send you some stamps."

"It's right in there between Mali and Dahomey." The captain began drawing excitedly with his finger on the steamy pilothouse windows. "Sierra Leone's down here, see, then Liberia and the Ivory Coast, then Ghana, Togo. You can't miss it." Saying the names, he seemed about to lapse into song. "If I could go to just five countries I've got stamps from, I'd die happy. I've never in my life been anyplace where if you pissed on the ground it wouldn't run into this river."

"The beautiful river," Jason murmured.

"To you, maybe. What I see is a thousand-mile sewer. An oily highway."

"That's what *Ohio* means in Iroquois. *Beautiful river.*"

The captain grunted. "You read a lot, don't you?"

"Life would be awfully pale without books."

"I know what you mean," said the captain vaguely. "Tell me, how'd you get started in this traveling business?"

Not used to answering personal questions, Jason was slow to respond. In Buddha, people thought of him as a two-legged calculator, without memory for anything but numbers. "When I was nine years old," he said at last, "the librarian gave me a book about world religions. In it, I discovered that a famous Indian holy man had been named Buddha about a thousand years before anyone ever heard of America or Indiana, let alone our little town. And right then I realized how big a place the world is."

"You ought to collect stamps," said the captain.

"I detasseled corn in the summer and saved up enough money to buy an atlas. And I started planning this trip."

"So if you'd come from a place called Jonesville or Gnawbone you might never have stirred from home?"

"Quite possibly."

Rain had turned the bargeloads of coal as slick and lethal-looking as obsidian. Studying the captain's stamps, each one opening like a tiny window onto jungles and snowy mountains, Jason already felt a long way from home.

"Aren't you afraid of getting lost?" said the captain.

"I have a keen sense of smell," Jason replied. "I can tell you, for instance, that somewhere not far upriver there's a glue factory. And I've studied nature's signs on the weekends."

"Nature's signs?" the captain muttered.

Jason would not be daunted. He knew what he knew. Spiders build their webs in line with the wind. In deserts at sundown flocks of pigeons will lead you to a waterhole. Termite hills in Australia are topped by sharp ridges that point unerringly north and south. A darkness in the clouds above an ice-covered sea betrays open water. From walking in the Hoosier National Forest and from reading the journals of great explorers, Jason had learned such things and a thousand things more. At lunch, every working day for twenty-six years, he had studied the *National Geographic* and *Natural History* and the *Smithsonian*, so he knew how various parts of the world should look. He would be certain of recognizing a place when he came to it.

In Pittsburgh, Jason thanked the captain and continued eastward. Wishing to give his new boots a test, he refused all rides. He stopped shaving and his beard came in pale yellow, the color of old sheets. Every few hours, crossing Pennsylvania by the National Road, he consulted the map to see how far he still had to go to reach Philadelphia. The map, which he had picked up free at a gas station, was devoted to the Eastern United States. Being so ambitious in scope, it lacked details. For example, it made no mention of the Allegheny Mountains, over which he had been laboring for three days, and it neglected all rivers smaller than the Susquehanna. The atlas was too bulky to pack, but fortunately Jason had committed most of it to memory.

A rainstorm drove him to shelter on the porch of a farmhouse near Gettysburg. The only person home was a teenage girl who wore an actual bonnet. While brewing him a pot of sassafras tea, she told how her favorite pony had died from eating green apples. "Just swole up and keeled over," she said. Ever since the death of that pony she had been looking for another one just as small, as shaggy, and the same rusty color. A person could find such ponies on the Shetland Islands, or so she heard tell.

"If you pass by that way," she said to Jason, "and if you'd pick me out a mare that's less than ten hands high, with bushy mane and forelock down over its eyes, the color of this corduroy," giving him a scrap of cloth, "my daddy would pay for it and I'd put you in my prayers from now till eternity."

Jason wrote all the details in his notebook and tucked the piece of rust-colored cloth in his pocket. On the steps of the farmhouse as he was leaving, the girl handed him a corn bread muffin. He carried away with him the smell of her hair, like newly-cut pine boards.

Before he reached Philadelphia, where he stood on Penn's Landing beside the Delaware listening to a brass band play salsa tunes, three more people had charged him with missions. In addition to the chickens in Japan, postage stamps in Upper Volta, and ponies in the

Shetlands, there was a grave to be located in Belgium, a prison warden to interrogate in Mongolia, and a debt to collect in Malaysia. Jason was beginning to feel as though he had undertaken this journey on behalf of a multitude.

When the brass band crashed to its finale, the conductor, a dark-skinned man in a shirt embroidered with parrots, noticed him listening with rapt attention.

"If you think that was good," said the conductor, swaggering up to Jason, "you should hear the stuff we play on the ship."

The ship turned out to be the *Mexico* from Venezuela, a sailing schooner with three masts, bound on a training cruise to Europe. The musicians had been packed along to shorten the days with their playing. Jason arrived there with the band after an interlude in a seaman's bar, where he drank only apple juice.

"Not even a little beer, the man is so incorruptible!" the band leader proclaimed, introducing him to the first mate. "He will go with us to Portugal, no? A moral influence!"

The mate had no objections. Jason unrolled his sleeping bag on the deck, between two coils of rope.

Aside from the conductor and the first mate, no one on board spoke English. Jason managed quite well with gestures. His hands wove pictures in the air, and his face, once he relaxed a bit, had a mime's expressiveness. Encouraged by this show of understanding, the men approached him one by one, cooks and trombone-players and cabin boys, each one telling his life story in patient Spanish. Occasionally Jason would understand one of their questions well enough to record it in his notebook. Much of the time he simply nodded, absorbing their griefs and desires.

"You have sympathetic ears," the conductor crooned. "I can tell by the way you listen to our music."

They docked in New York, to replenish their supply of remedies for seasickness. Jason was glad of the stopover. He wanted to see the Empire State Building, because the limestone for constructing it had been quarried just down the road from his home in Indiana. Half a dozen sailors insisted on going with him, to protect him from thugs. They wore white, dazzling in the sunshine, and Jason dressed in his usual green. The ascent in the elevator made him dizzy. From the top of the Empire State Building he looked down at the lesser skyscrapers, the maze of streets, the hurry of people, and thought of the quarries near Buddha. It seemed a strange thing, to dig so much limestone out of the earth, drag it halfway across the country, and stack it so high in the air. The sailors dared one another to throw coins from the roof. Jason cautioned them against it, for he had read that a penny dropped from such a height could pierce right through a person's skull. The sailors understood his gestures, if not his words, and put their hands in their pockets.

On a street near the docks a barefooted woman asked Jason to help find her baby. The sailors joined in the search, peering through gratings in the sidewalk, turning over heaps of rags in doorways, but they could discover no baby, and at length the woman went sniffling away. Even lacking several teeth and smelling of cough medicine, she made Jason's heart ache.

After three panhandlers had shuffled up to him begging money and a wino had asked him for advice about delirium, the sailors perceived that Jason was a man who drew other people's needs to him as a magnet draws the inner spirits of iron. Once this was clear to them, they formed a barricade around him and let no one through. And so they arrived back at the ship, the sailors in their white suits encircling him like a picket fence, green-clad Jason in the middle like a rare plant.

Sight of the Atlantic Ocean made Lake Michigan shrink in his memory to the size of a puddle. During the first night at sea, Jason lay awake thinking about the spaces between stars. Things were so far apart in the universe, it was a wonder to him that any two atoms ever rubbed against one another. That all the stuff necessary for making his body had drifted together within this immensity seemed to him wildly improbable. And yet here he was, a bony lump of flesh, nauseous from the heaving of the sea. He sniffed avidly at a land-breeze, which carried the reek of an oil refinery and a pig farm. So long as he could smell the shore he was not utterly adrift in this emptiness. During the day he gained comfort from watching the gulls and terns cruising in the wake of the ship, but eventually these birds reached the border of their fishing territory and swooped back.

Whenever the sea was calm enough the band set up folding chairs on deck and played music, either feverish dance tunes or mournful ballads, depending on the mood of the conductor. The off-duty sailors hunkered down beside Jason and resumed their life stories. Every now and again he would scribble a memorandum in his notebook: *Greetings from Juan to Esmerelda in Istanbul,* it might be, or, *Check on price of garnets in Turkestan.* When the sailors arrived in bunches and were too shy to speak of what pressed on their hearts, Jason entertained them by calculating the hour of moonrise and moonset. At night he would estimate the time by reckoning from the position of stars. Of course they had tables for predicting the movements of the moon and they had luminous watches for telling the time, yet they were fascinated by Jason's ability to compute these things in his head.

"Sailors should know such tricks," he scolded. "What if you were cast adrift in a lifeboat, and nothing but your wits to guide you?"

With his odd notions about seacraft, his habit of sheltering beneath a fern-colored umbrella, and his energetic pantomimes, this gringo was the most engaging performer they had ever brought on board. Even the band was dull by comparison. The conductor soon grew jealous, and regretted having offered Jason a ride. But the other musicians were secretly pleased, for they would rather confess their miseries to Jason in the shade of his umbrella than blow on their horns in the sun. They were glum when he strode down the gangplank in Lisbon. Even the conductor, repenting of his jealousy, wept a few tears. The cook chased after him with a savory parcel. Jason tipped his green slouch hat to them and headed off walking across Europe.

If he kept on course as far as the Bering Strait, he would cover twelve thousand miles before reaching another ocean. To keep track of his progress he stuffed a handful of pebbles into his left pocket. Each time his left foot struck the ground for the hundredth time, he moved a pebble to the right pocket. For every ten pebbles thus transferred he would have walked about a mile. After two days he grew weary of such counting, however, and decided to walk on in ignorance of distances.

His dramatic gestures served him well in Portugal and Spain. Three days out from Lisbon, a peasant gave him a ride on a donkey, unlashing a brace of water pots to make room. Jason had never sat astride a beast before, not even at the Lawrence County Fair, where he went each July to admire the champion rabbits and bulls. Riding the donkey was a bit like sailing, and inspired in him the same glee, as if he were playing a trick on the laws of physics. He slept in a hut with the peasant, staying an extra day in order to figure the man's income taxes. For supper each night they ate a flat bread which reminded Jason by its smell of the chicken lady, Doris Wilkins. One of the man's children asked him in textbook English if he would kindly secure the autograph of a soccer star in Brazil. To be certain of the spelling, Jason had the boy write the hero's name in his notebook.

For several days, as he trudged across the desolate plains of northern Spain, the Pyrenees loomed out of the north like a bank of thunderclouds. Jason rode across the mountains in the truck of a painter who was smuggling marijuana into France. "With the stink of turpentine," the painter confided, "the dogs cannot smell my weeds."

Neither dogs nor border guards had any chance of sniffing this delivery, in any case, because the painter veered off the road on the French side of the mountains and bounced the last few miles across a rutted field. "Is it true the Colombian gold leaf is sweeter than our Spanish?" the smuggler wanted to know.

Jason explained that he had never smoked any variety of leaf, but offered to seek the opinion of experts.

The smuggler's family turned out to be Loyalists who had been hiding in the south of France since the Spanish Civil War. They gave him the names of other old guerrillas, with addresses ranging across Europe from Toulouse to Bucharest. "Kiss Vladimir in Odessa for me," said the smuggler's wife.

In order to accommodate the names and addresses, Jason had to buy a second notebook. By the time he reached Vienna he was writing in his third. For many of the questions he had been asked along the way he had already found answers. These he wrote carefully on postcards, which he mailed to the questioners. Although the drift of his travels had carried him past Africa, he had found in Geneva a packet of stamps from Upper Volta, a present for the captain of the coal barge. He bought a Shetland pony of just the right color from a circus in Lichtenstein and had it shipped to the girl in Pennsylvania.

Every day or so he would knock at a door—in Berchtesgaden, say, or Zagreb, sometimes at a farm in the middle of nowhere—to pass along a message. A seamstress in Milan was so astonished to find this green, backpacked apparition on her doorstep that she knelt down and uttered a prayer. When he delivered news of her son, who was earning good money at a fish cannery and had given up drink, she made Jason stay with her for three days so that all her relatives might hear from his very lips these revelations about her wandering boy. "You see," she crowed, "he doesn't take after his good-for-nothing father!"

As Jason was leaving she hung a silver whistle on a thong about his neck. "If you're ever lost or in danger, blow this like fury and God will save you."

The only danger he encountered in Vienna was the loveliness of the women. He could not understand how their husbands and boy-friends managed to stroll beside them without breaking into shouts. He would have shouted, if he had been permitted so much as to hold one of those women by the hand. Watching them feeding seals in the zoo or tying the knots of kerchiefs beneath their exquisite chins, he was struck again by the improbability of the universe. Nothing in books explained how the sight of a face could set up these enormous tides in his heart.

The women had so disturbed his equilibrium that he nearly forgot to buy a pound of chocolate from a certain confectioner in Vienna for a policeman in Madrid. The main post office happened to be just across the street from the confectioner's. While he was mailing the chocolate, he decided on an impulse to ask the postmistress if there were any general delivery letters for him. No one on earth knew he would pass through Vienna—or even cared, for that matter—and yet asking for general delivery seemed the sort of thing a serious traveler should do. The woman soon returned with a postcard. On one side it bore a photograph of the limestone pyramid under construction in Bedford, Indiana, right near his hometown, and on the other side a printed message: MR. MOSS, I'LL MEET YOU IN TOKYO, IN FRONT OF THE ASSYRIAN EXILE CHURCH, THE FIRST OF MAY AT HIGH NOON. WE'LL CHECK OUT THOSE JAPANESE CHICK-ENS TOGETHER. HOPE YOU'RE HAVING A GOOD TRIP. YOUR ITCHY-FOOTED FRIEND, DORIS WILKINS. In the upper left corner a forceful hand had written, "Number 212 of 500."

Jason recalled with perfect clarity jouncing in the truck beside the bearish widow who ranted in rage and affection about her four children and her farm mortgage and her fool husband who had died under five yards of concrete, and behind her voice the groan of the engine and the squawking of hens, and her nearness filling the cab like the aroma of hot biscuits. Merely thinking about it, here on the tile floor of a Vienna post office, he was pierced by longing.

Of course he could not possibly meet her in Tokyo. Would she expect him to shake hands? Kiss her? Buy her lunch? He was too old for learning the do-si-do of courtship.

Yet he held off replying to her message. Each time he entered a post office, instead of mailing the letter of apology which he had laboriously composed, he inquired at the general delivery counter. There were postcards waiting for him in every capital and in many of the secondary cities. One side invariably showed the limestone pyramid, the other carried the familiar message from Doris Wilkins. The only change from card to card was the number.

By the time he reached Ankara, where he collected his twenty-seventh card, Jason realized that he could not mail his letter of apology. He would have to meet the chicken lady. She had gone to so much trouble, and had perhaps already begun studying Japanese in preparation for her trip. Even now, browsing through catalogs, she might be circling the photographs of items she would need. Thinking about her preparations, he recovered some of his own early excitement, almost as if he himself were setting out on a journey once again.

For the truth was, his knees throbbed, his boots had worn thin, his umbrella was springing leaks. After tramping only a quarter of the way around the world, his joints were beginning to sound like old staircases. At least he remembered to rub alcohol into the soles of his feet. This not only prevented blisters but also mitigated the smell, a welcome side effect, for he was often forced to go long stretches without a bath.

In Kabul, a shoemaker to whom he had delivered a recipe for mutton pie rewarded him with a pair of oxhide boots, and also mended his umbrella. "To protect you from the murderous sun," the shoemaker signaled in gestures.

Jason had chosen to contend with sun instead of snow, taking a southerly route through Asia in order to avoid the Russian winter. This forced him to neglect a good many of the memoranda in his notebooks, including that troublesome kiss which he was supposed to award in Odessa. But what more could he do? How was one man to run errands for the entire world?

The new oxhide boots and the restored umbrella—as well as, he had to admit, the prospect of meeting Doris Wilkins in Tokyo—stirred up his spirits. He crossed northern Pakistan in a jeep with an army patrol, thus saving his legs a good deal of stony walking. The soldiers advised him against entering India. The beggars and fake holy men in that land would nibble him to nothing. "There is a glow about you which the needy can detect from miles away," said the lieutenant, who then asked Jason if he would mind carrying a blood-stained handkerchief to an old war comrade in Tibet. "He will know what it means," the lieutenant added darkly.

Although Jason kept taking on small items for delivery, such as this handkerchief, or a comb from a matron in Damascus, a pair of false teeth from a fisherman in Beirut, a harmonica from a streetsweeper in Sofia, he also gave away to urchins some of the equipment which he had brought along, and so the weight of his backpack did not vary much up or down. As soon as he delivered anything—the goblet for a Greek Orthodox priest in Baghdad, for example—someone else was sure to give him a new parcel.

The beggars and holy men did indeed flock to him in India, but instead of asking for handouts they asked for advice. They perceived that he was a battered pilgrim, a veteran of untold miles, and wanted to know what visions seized him when the winds turned wicked or rains filled the sky or the sun squatted for hours on a mountain peak. Jason gave the best answers he could. The children toyed with his compass, squealing and leaping about to avoid the magical point of its needle. The old men tried on his felt hat solemnly, sniffing the headband, examining the pattern of sweat stains as if it were some obscure calligraphy.

Here in the land of the original Buddha, Jason shrugged off his weariness. He climbed through a mountain pass into Tibet, in company with a band of refugees from Bangladesh. All night they sang folk songs as they walked, and Jason hummed along. One by one they sidled up to him and showed him an old scar, a tattoo, or merely tramped beside him in deep silence, occasionally brushing their fingers against his sleeves. When an avalanche threatened to bury their little party, he remembered the silver whistle hanging round his neck and gave it a powerful puff. As the snow crashed down harmlessly behind them, the refugees decided that Jason was indeed a wayfaring saint. How else explain the odd parchment color of his skin, the unruly beard, the walking stick that became a tent, the tamed avalanche?

Runners carried the news ahead into the hinterlands of Tibet. In the villages, children made him presents of flowers. The elders pressed their foreheads to his and clasped him gravely by the hand. Girls fed him fragrant beans wrapped in leaves. Word of him traveled ahead to the Chinese border guards, who gave him a bamboo flute and escorted him to the nearest communal farm. There he was examined minutely by dozens of furtive eyes. Very little in his appearance fit their notions of how a man should look. They did not believe in saints, but knew all about wandering wise men, and took him for one. To entertain them, Jason recounted his entire journey in mime. The children clapped their hands and rocked on their heels. The old people chewed smilingly on sticks.

When it was time for him to leave, a doctor on a bicycle led him to the next commune, and from there two girls led him to the next, and thus he was guided from settlement to settlement across China, telling in each place the story of his travels. The number of companions escorting him between villages kept growing, until by the time he reached Lanzhou, where another card from Doris awaited him, he was marching along at the head of a parade. Although he could not play any musical instrument, he boldly whistled along on his bamboo flute. His followers imagined that the awful noise he made was music in his native land.

In Xi'an he delivered a paper fan, in Nanjing a pair of sandals encrusted with seashells, in Shanghai a drop of amber enshrining a flea. As he completed each errand he placed an X in the margin of his notebook. No sooner did he complete a task, however, than somebody would set him a new one. Even as he began inscribing memoranda in his seventh notebook, Jason thought back with pleasure over his modest labors, which had now been scattered halfway around the world.

The throngs who accompanied him into Shanghai gave the local authorities a fright. Was it an invasion? Refugees from some disaster in the interior? Spying Jason, they were reassured. Such a man could not march at the head of anything dangerous. The mayor, learning that this serene stranger was bound for Tokyo, asked him to deliver a copper thimble to her cousin. Since the mayor's brother piloted a fishing boat, Jason's passage to Japan was quickly arranged.

In the waters off Kyushu the Chinese rowed him to a Japanese trawler, which carried him into Tokyo Bay on the last day of April. The sea journey restored him completely. He drank jasmine tea and mended his gear. While the fishermen labored, he studied the flight of birds and the motions of clouds and the colors of the waves, getting his bearings in the great wheel of things. To keep his joints limber he stood up from time to time and danced on the deck, or acted out some portion of his travels for the fishermen.

The woman in Tokyo to whom he delivered the thimble put him up for the night in her paper-walled house. "The honorable sir is truly around the world going?" she asked in polite disbelief.

"Yes, indeed," said Jason, "and I'm on the homeward leg."

The woman's knowledge of English stopped short of allowing her to understand how a trip could be divided into legs, and so she merely smiled, a disarming smile which left Jason wondering how he could possibly gather up enough courage before tomorrow noon to meet the chicken lady.

That evening he counted his postcards: sixty-three photos of the Indiana pyramid, sixty-three identical messages from Doris Wilkins. Nothing in the whole journey so amazed him as his arrival here for this rendezvous. He was sorely tempted to blow on his whistle; and indeed that night, in the midst of a dream about flower-covered islands, he did so, waking not only his hosts but also the neighboring families, all of whom shuffled into his sleeping alcove to see what was the matter.

"A dream," Jason apologized.

Staring down into his eyes, as if inspecting a lake for turtles, an old woman declared, "It is the love ache." Everyone in the room nodded agreement.

Next morning, as he walked the last few blocks to the Assyrian Exile Church, Jason felt himself laboring uphill, even though the land was perfectly flat. He reached the spot five minutes early. Doris was already there, gazing about at the pedestrians as if they were migrating caribou.

"You don't look half bad," she cried on catching sight of him. "In fact, you look like you've opened up to the sunshine. I do like that beard. Who'd ever think it would come out like new butter? How're the legs?"

"Still kicking," said Jason. He was trying to decide whether to doff his hat or shake her hand when she seized him in a mighty hug and planted a kiss on his chapped lips.

"So you got my card?" she said, releasing him.

"Oh, yes. Several times. Sixty-three times, in fact."

"I sent five hundred. Didn't want to miss you, and God only knew where you might be headed. You were pretty vague about your itinerary, back when you hitched a ride in my truck."

She was dressed in gear to match his own, except in yellow instead of green, floppy hat and windbreaker and baggy trousers, a rucksack with sleeping bag strapped on, a walking stick that doubled as an umbrella, a canteen slung round her neck. Out of respect for her stout build and burly manner, the pedestrians gave her a wide berth, swerving to either side as if she were a boulder in their path.

"Who's looking after the chickens?" Jason inquired.

"My brother. He owes me a favor for pasturing his goats on my land."

"And the children? Four of them, if I remember correctly?"

"Four is right. Seems like forty, some days. They're with my other brother, who promised to keep them until school starts in September. I've been feeding him and his family free eggs ever since Adam and Eve got kicked out of the garden."

Jason reflected on dates for a moment, then asked, "You're planning to be away from home until September?"

"I don't see how we can get back to Buddha any sooner, not if we're going to really see South America."

"Right," said Jason, after the shock had worn off.

Before shipping to South America, they walked and rode the

length of Japan, investigating numerous breeds of chickens along the way. Although some varieties were indeed quieter than the ones Doris raised, none laid as well or put on flesh as quickly, and so she decided to stick with what she had.

"There's no substitute for looking into things yourself," she declared.

Among the other things they looked into while traversing Japan were volcanoes, about which Jason had often read in the *National Geographic*. He felt some kinship with these quaking mountains, for ever since joining company with Doris he had been feeling as though a pool of lava bubbled in his own depths.

Although Doris rode guard beside him, people still approached him daily with petitions. Would he carry a deathbed message from a grandfather to a grandson? Would he give a wedding certificate to a plumber? Would he pass along a poem to an estranged sister? Filled with these missions, his notebooks occupied the lower third of his pack.

"Folks know a soft touch when they see one," said Doris.

"I can't help it," he said.

"Don't try. I've lived too long around people you couldn't rouse with a poker."

She made no bones about anything, eating out of the same bowl with him, unrolling her sleeping bag next to his at night. She treated their journeying together as such a matter of course, a thing as natural as summer grasshoppers, that after a while Jason began to treat it so himself. In fact, the second night of their passage from Japan to Argentina, he was the one who finally zipped their sleeping bags together. They rode on a freighter as guests of the bosun, to whom they had delivered a family watch. Although loaded now with automobiles, the freighter smelled of the cattle it always carried on the return trip from Argentina.

"For warmth," Jason said, explaining the joined bags.

Doris required no explanations. She crawled in beside him and threw a brawny arm across his throat, as though dragging him to shore, then she led him down into the lava depths of his body and back up again, up into the avenues of birds, up into the moon's path, up where the edges of constellations brushed against one another in the invincible darkness.

"I don't care about marrying," said Doris, as they started their hike northward from Buenos Aires. "But I wouldn't mind some company. I just got to feeling closed in and smothered, the way I was living. And it wasn't only from breathing feathers. If you want, I'll handle the chickens and you can do your bookkeeping in the dining room."

"That sounds good to me," Jason replied.

"How do you feel about kids?"

"I've met some amazing ones on this trip."

"Good, because mine would amaze even a zoo keeper." She heaved a sigh. "Someday maybe they'll quit going to university and get jobs. They've got so many degrees now, if they could turn them in for a nickel each we could all retire."

Jason and Doris traveled the length of the continent, through swamps and deserts, with gauchos and priests and tax-collectors, sometimes in the cabooses of trains, in pirogues and panel trucks, once on an ox cart, twice on mules, moving steadily northward until they reached the jungles of Central America. From there they took ship to New Orleans and then worked their way up the Mississippi Valley, Jason distributing messages and presents. They hiked from Illinois into Indiana, then rode the last fifty miles into Buddha with a bus full of gospel singers who were on their way to a contest in Fort Wayne.

The town was unchanged by the passage of a year, but Jason surveyed it now with altered eyes. Gas station, liquor store, corner grocery, rival churches, nothing had budged an inch. Some of last year's posters, faded by sunlight, still hung in windows. The same flowers were blooming in front yards. The money he had counted for others still swam like fish from pocket to pocket. Familiar voices complained of familiar ailments, or shouted with familiar joys. It was a spot on earth. Just one spot. He had dozens of errands still to run, parcels to deliver, questions to answer.

"I don't think I'll be able to stay here long," Jason confessed.

"I didn't expect you would," Doris answered.

He stared grimly at the buckled sidewalks and potholed streets, the pathways of his old self. Beside him, Doris seemed to glow in her yellow traveling clothes.

"Are your kids big enough to fend for themselves?" he said.

"If they aren't now, they never will be," she replied.

"Then you're free to go?"

"Free as a bluejay."

That night they hunched over the atlas and studied maps, their shoulders drifting together like the curves of continents.

I Can If I May

James Alexander Thom

Dear God up in heaven, don't let them make fun of me.
I don't want them to look at me or say anything. Amen.
And don't let Mother get mad at me for this. Amen again.

SCOTTY prayed it hard enough that he could feel the tickly feeling in his chest.

(Snicket, snicket, snicket)

"Cut it like my father's," he, the chaplain's boy, had said.

When the barber made the comb and the scissors go up the back of the neck it made the tickly feeling on the outside, like the tickly feeling on the inside when God listened to his prayers.

Mr. Skaggs the barber had pumped his foot on a pedal and the chair had gone *psss psss psss* and up so that Scotty sat way up high with a striped sheet over all of him except his head and when the chair would go around he would see his head in the mirror.

(Snicket, snicket)

Mr. Skaggs breathed loudly through his nosehair. His hands were white with long black hair on their fingers, his little finger sticking out straight when he snicked the scissors. It tickled and made goose bumps.

There were soapy smells like the smell of things in the medicine cabinet at home in the bathroom. The barbershop bathroom was stinky and had hard bugs, and the farmers always left globs of tobacco

43

and chewed parts of cigars on its linoleum floor. One time when his mother had brought him to the barbershop he had had to go to the bathroom and it was horrible and he had been afraid to sit down. He never would go again in the bathroom here. He would do it at home before he came here.

The big men in the chairs around the room watched the barber cut the curly hair of the chaplain's boy. Some of them looked as if they were way far back behind their eyes looking out at him and they didn't ever smile except when they laughed loud and mean-sounding. Whenever they talked, it was about President Roosevelt and crops and programs, and some unknowable thing called the Grange, and other things he didn't understand.

He didn't like to look at those men.

I wonder if they have souls, he thought. They don't ever shine their shoes and they wear bib overalls like the ones I used to wear in the pictures Father took of me before I went to kindergarten.

Farmers ride on tractors but some of them have horses with long hair on their ankles and they put iron shoes on their feet with nails. It must hurt to have nails driven in your feet. A horse up by the feed store blew his nose at me this morning.

Scotty had heard boys at school say that Mr. Skaggs the barber was in something called the kay kay kay and once he had caught a nigger man and cut his ear off with a straight razor. Scotty was careful not to think of that when he had to come to the barbershop. The kay kay kay was another of those unknowable things.

It was scary to come here. But Mr. Skaggs was the only barber in the town.

The barbershop floor had some of the hair off of everybody in town on it, hair from farmers and Mister Green the banker and the school principal and Link Bemis the garage man, and now Scotty's own curls.

Mother has a piece of my hair in the back of a gold thing on her necklace and she thinks it's important but there's a lot more of mine here on the floor and I wonder if she would want it because I could take her lots of it.

(Clicket, clicket, clicket)

The barber cut the chaplain's boy's hair in the front and the hair fell on eyelashes and nose and down on the striped sheet and into the sunshine on the floor.

He's cutting it awful short.

Mother is going to be mad at me. Father might like it because it's going to be like his Army haircut but Mother is going to be awful mad at me.

I wonder how you're ever supposed to know what's right and what's wrong.

The brush tickled over his ears and the new nakedness of his neck. A dry fog of lilac powder swirled. The farmers now were reading newspapers in their waiting chairs around the wall and drawling among themselves about the White River bottomlands and about croup and hives and trotline fishing. They weren't looking at him now, and he didn't want them to. But then Mr. Skaggs said loudly:

"By gollies, there! Now if y' don't look like a little sojer instead of that Shirley Temple in the pitcher show!"

Everybody in the shop looked up over the edges of the newspapers at him. Wheezes and cackles of laughter echoed around the room and the boy wanted to cringe down and hide inside the barber's cloth.

Then the room swung quickly around and he was looking past Mr. Skaggs's shoulder and the tan-stained stone sink and the hair-oil bottles, at the big mirror. His face was blurred by tears of embarrassment, a pale little oval among pearly white reflections, patches of murk and light, dark squares and glints. He could feel the men's stares on the back of his neck and scalp and he wanted to be away from the barbershop.

"Well, whatcha think, Little Sojer?" said the barber at his side.

"Thank you, sir." His voice was small and quavery among the darkly rumbling voices of the men in the room. Then he was swung around again and he felt the cloth unpinned at his neck, saw it whipped aside, saw the corduroy of his pants and saw the yellow curls of his hair fall among the dark straight oily clippings on the white six-sided tiles of the floor. The chair descended in squishy jerks and Mr. Skagg's hand closed around his upper arm to help him step down from the curlicued iron footrest of the chair. His knees were trembling, his feet yearning toward the worn wooden sun-baked threshold. Across the room a farmer had risen from his chair and was coming toward him. The man's denim overalls, wash-pale on the thighs, frayed cuffs knotted with mud and manure, moved past toward the barber chair. He smelled like the stuff Scotty's mother used in mop water to kill germs. Scotty shied aside, sorting through the belongings in his pockets. He withdrew a half dollar, which he put in the barber's palm. The barber rang the cash register and returned two dimes and a nickel.

"Thank you, Mr. Skaggs, sir."

"Welcome. And y'all come back when you get some more of them curls growed out. You're 'bout the only customer I got that ain't on the cuff."

"Yessir," the boy said, wondering what that meant. Then he walked as calmly as he could to the door, stepped off the threshold into the dry yellow sunlight and broke into a sprint along the cracked sidewalk, past the ten-cent store and the drugstore, then diagonally across the town's one main intersection, and stopped in the shade of the old brick bank with the boards over its windows.

It was done. He had made his first trip alone to the barbershop and he had told the barber, proud and excited and scared:

"Please cut it like my father's, sir."

"Are you sure?" the barber had asked.

"Yessir."

Now he wondered what his mother would say, and was afraid of going home. He walked slowly, dragging his feet, along Main Street toward his house. He thought that he should not go home. He wondered if he could stay away from home until his hair would grow back out, but decided it would be too many days. He came to the open door of the grocery. From its dark interior came the scents of smoked hams and fresh onions and kerosene and some sweet odors of ripe fruits. Just within the door there was a covered glass jar of twisted licorice whips. Inside the window there was a quart jar full of pinto beans, with a sign beside it: GUESS HOW MANY BEANS IN THIS JAR WIN 25¢

"You may get candy with the change from your haircut," his mother had told him. But he didn't want the grocer or anybody to see him the way he looked now.

The grass and weeds were yellow and hot in the empty lot next to the old red brick Moose Lodge. The lodge's two high windows looked out over the dry, bug-shrilling weeds from under brick arches like eyebrows. He stood in the lot near the dusty hollyhocks, toeing a rusted barrel hoop, miserable, intimidated by the dull red ugly countenance of the mysterious lodge. Whatever it was that had made him afraid of the eyes of the unsmiling men in the barbershop had always made him afraid of the gaunt black windows. A breath of air moved around his head and he smelled the faint lilac of the barber's dusting powder. He lowered his gaze to the poor and pebbly earth under the plantain and dandelion and thistle and, for the first time, moved his hand up to feel his hair. His palm felt the soft pliant bristle with the skull so smooth and close under it. He jerked his hand away. He felt strange, as if he might either cry or throw up.

It doesn't feel like my father's hair at all, he thought. His stands up straight and is penny-colored and springy under your fingers and shaved off everywhere except on the top of his head and it feels good to touch. His is an Army haircut but I don't feel like a soldier. I feel like a dumb little poop, he thought. I wish I could make it be this morning again and then I wouldn't go in and say, Please cut it like my father's.

Somewhere close by, a cat began squalling, over and over, a very loud and wild and hurting sound. It made his back tingle. He walked out of the weedy lot and turned left into the alley that led to his home. Mrs. Franklin's privy stood in the sun buzzing with flies and he held his breath when he went past it. The screeching of the cat sounded as if it were coming from there. From inside the outhouse. Scotty stopped at the pitch barrel behind Bemis's Garage. He stood in the alley and listened to the clangor of hammering inside the garage where Mr. Link Bemis, the town's only mechanic, labored in greasy shadow. The cat was still screaming from the privy. Scotty took his pocketknife, his bone-handled Barlow, out of his pocket, opened it, and carved a morsel of pitch out of the barrel. He chewed it, and thought of the chant he and Mackie Townsend had made up:

Chew on pitch and your teeth won't itch.

The terrible cat-screams went on. It was not the low ghostly noise a cat makes when it wants to get with another cat, but instead seemed to be the sound of an animal fighting for its life. It made the new-shaved skin of his neck cold and crawly. He wanted to go and see what was wrong but was held back by a dread of what he might see. The iron hammering in Mr. Bemis's shop had stopped, and the screams of the cat now seemed to be the center of the world. Scotty went trembling toward the sound, that sound which scraped his soul now like the sound of fingernails on the blackboard at school.

The door of Mrs. Franklin's privy was open and the screams were coming from inside. Scotty looked into the darkness and saw a boy with black hair, in a red shirt, standing in the privy, facing the seat, holding a rope high in front of him with both hands. The rope hung down into the hole in the toilet seat and it was jerking and twitching. The cat's yowls seemed to be coming from the hole, and it was a moment before Scotty could understand that the cat must be hanging at the end of that rope, down in that awful place below the toilet seat.

Two things happened in the moment of his understanding. The door of Mrs. Franklin's house squealed and slammed, and the boy holding the rope turned and saw Scotty staring in the privy door at him, mouth agape and eyes wide.

The boy holding the rope was Billy Bob Skaggs, the barber's son. He was three years older than Scotty, was doing his second year in the second grade, and was feared by almost every boy in the school. He was big for his nine years and hard-fisted. He had knocked out the front teeth of several younger children with his knuckles, and some older ones too, and once had broken a teacher's glasses with a rock from his powerful slingshot.

Scotty stood frozen. Billy Bob's pale gray eyes rested on him for an instant, wild and glinting, then darted over his shoulder toward the sound of someone's approach. Mrs. Franklin's querulous voice was coming among the tall hollyhocks. Scotty could hear it between the squalls of the cat.

Suddenly Scotty found himself holding the end of the jerking rope, which Billy Bob had thrust into his hand.

"Kid," Billy Bob's voice hissed in his face, "you ever tell anyone and I'll cut your ear off!"

Then he was gone with a rustle through the weeds and flower stalks.

And when Mrs. Franklin's big old body loomed in the privy door, shutting off the afternoon sun, Scotty was standing there totally bewildered, clutching the rope, a hideous threat still sounding in his ears, watching the slimy forepaws of the cat come scrabbling and clawing out of the hole, then the filth-soaked dark head with its crazed yellow eyes blinking. "Scott Montgomery! What on earth!" Mrs. Franklin cried. And at that moment, the reeking, dripping animal attained the edge of the seat and launched itself with claws bared toward what it thought was its tormentor. Scotty dropped the end of the rope with a screech and ducked, and the snarling, spitting demon, the besmirched noose still hanging from its neck, struck Mrs. Franklin full on the bosom, tore at her white blouse for a second, then sprang off and vanished into the brush with a rasping wail. Mrs. Franklin stumbled backward and fell among the hollyhocks.

And Scotty, in a blind terror, crashed through the lilac bushes to the alley and ran. The cries of Mrs. Franklin faded behind him.

Under the grape arbor in the side yard the shaded grass was long and clean-smelling. Laddie, the family's collie, slept beside his doghouse at the far corner of the yard. Scotty lay on his stomach with his chin on his fist and looked through the vine leaves at the gray-shuttered parlor window of his white house. Faintly he could hear his mother's voice and Mrs. Franklin's voice coming from within. Their voices went up and down, as if they were arguing.

He took the wad of chewed pitch out of his mouth and pressed it against an upright of the grape arbor. His jaws had grown tired from chewing it for so long.

After a while he heard his mother and Mrs. Franklin talking on the front porch, then the front screen door slapped and Mrs. Franklin marched down the sidewalk with the blue shadows of the green maple leaves sliding back over her white blouse. The front of the blouse was covered with brown smudges.

About five minutes later, Scotty's mother came out of the side door and looked around. He ducked deeper into the grass. He was afraid to let her see him. He sensed that he was in grave trouble.

Lying under the sheltering arbor, he folded his arms on the grass and put his face down against them and shuddered.

I hope Mother will believe me instead of Mrs. Franklin, he thought.

Then he had an awful feeling. He *couldn't* tell her what had really happened. Billy Bob Skaggs would cut off his ear if he did!

Scotty lay in the shade for a long time. He was afraid to go in the house or go anywhere else in town. Billy Bob might be lurking up any alley or behind any shrub. Somehow all at once this had become the worst day Scotty had ever lived. There didn't seem to be any answer to his problem.

He wished his father were home from Fort Harrison. Then he thought of how angry he would be about this and was glad he wasn't.

Scotty woke up. He had dozed. The red and white stripes of his sleeves flowed together, shimmered, too close for focus. His feet touched the ground alternately, rhythmically, toe-down into the grass. His voice a thin and languid plaint in the vast buzzing brilliance of the summer afternoon, he began to chant, just above a whisper, in the narrow cool confines of the grape leaves and grass, the soothing little song his mother had made up for him one day when he had been stubborn and disobedient:

> *"As a boy I say,*
> *I can if I may.*
> *But I'll say as a man:*
> *I may if I can."*

And drowsily he thought what that seemed to mean. Until you're a man somebody is supposed to tell you what's right and what's wrong. But when you're a man, you will have to know it yourself, and what you should do is what you can do.

But it was always hard to know what was right and wrong. Now knowing could make you sick.

Hues, greenish, reddish, whitish, yellowish, pinkish, skinnish, turned and changed in his drowsy eyes, spread long shines, folded under new shapes of color in his half-open lids, and his heart beat faster against the ground. A fly tickled his ear, an unbearably exquisite tickle, a skin-twitching tickle, said, nynynynynynynynynynynynyny, and went away. Again sleepiness flowed up from the earth into him through his elbows nose ears eyes mouth skin bellybutton doodly knees toes, coming in warm and fuzzy, tickly as if he were a fly tickling the earth and it him.

WHAK!

It was the side door screen door and it woke him, and when he looked up his mother was standing there in the sunlight, her hair very shiny light rich brown and her dress light blue with white lines, beyond the grape leaves, and she was looking toward him.

"Scotty. Will you please come in the house?"

And rising, full of richness from the ground, a very intriguing question in his mind, he started toward her, skipping.

"Mother, does a fly get tickled feet when he walks on my ear? Does he?"

"Oh, my heavens," she said with both hands suddenly at the sides of her face. "What on earth happened to your head?"

He had forgotten about that, the haircut. And about Billy Bob and the cat. Now all the bad things crowded up in his mind again and though he was looking down at the limestone flagstones white in the green grass he could see instead the strange sun-dark faces of the men in the barber shop and the mad cat covered with do-do. His heart hurt and there was something heavy in his back and legs and he knew somehow that he probably was going to tell a lie.

"Why did that man cut your hair all off? *Why* in the *world?*"

"I don't know," he lied. He had been ready to lie about the cat but was surprised to hear himself lie about the haircut. "I don't feel good."

"No wonder." Her eyes went terrible and he knew she now was thinking about what Mrs. Franklin had told her. He couldn't look at her face. The screen door and the white sides of the house and the blue flower-spikes on the mint beside the door were blurred in his sight. Strands of her hair stirred shining in the air and her flowery powdery scent came summerwarm from her dress. Her niceness that had always been there for him to go to now seemed to be over where he could not approach it, because of the things that had happened to him on this day. She was frowning.

"Your father'll be home Friday and he'll go down and find out why that barber did that to you," she said.

"Will I have to go with him when he goes?" Scotty asked, remembering that he had said, *Please cut it like my father's, sir.*

"We'll see." She walked around him and inspected him, sighing. "Now," she said. "I heard something so distressing about you today that I don't know quite how to deal with it. You know what I'm talking about, don't you?"

"No, 'm."

"Oh?" Her eyebrows went up and her eyelids grew hard and her mouth pursed. "I won't have any lying, Scotty. Not in this family. I'm talking about that perfectly dreadful matter about the cat."

"I didn't do anything, Mother."

"Oh? Then you're saying Mrs. Franklin lied to me? Careful now."

"Huh-uh. But she just didn't know what . . ." *I'll cut your ear off,* he remembered, and said no more.

"Lie to me and you'll go to bed without supper," she warned.

"I didn't do anything."

"Very well." She looked more hurt than angry. "We'll see Friday when your father gets home. No supper for you. Up to your room. You can come down when you're ready to tell me the truth."

Yellow sunheat fell behind as they stepped into the cool dimness of the kitchen and the screen door smacked. He went across the tile floor and up the hallway to the stairs, then up the dark varnished steps to his room.

The rug in his bedroom was dull blue and white with an Indian design in the border. The rug was very old with tan strings showing in it where the blue-and-white fuzz was worn down. Under the west window there was a dazzling square of sunlight and above it dust motes drifted.

He sat on the edge of his bed, wearing just his underpants, and looked at the rug. He could hear his mother walking around downstairs in the kitchen. The scent of cooking meat stole up the stairs. For several minutes then there was the clinking knocking regular sound as she shredded cabbage for slaw on that tin thing that cuts your knuckles up when you try it.

If she's still fixing supper, she must be expecting me to come down and tell her.

But I can't.

He knelt on the foot of the bed and put his hands on the footboard. He looked across at the mirror above the dresser. There were his small pale shoulders and the minute pink tips of what giggly DeeDee Willoughby the neighbor girl called titties, and there was his sturdy white neck and the face that looked so changed and strange and peeled. He felt coldish on his forehead and shoulders, and turned away and got down off the bed. He was afraid to lie down because he knew by the dizzy thing in his chest that if he did lie down and shut his eyes the bed would start whirling him around and make him urp.

He went to the window and stood there with the sunlight on him and his nose and forehead against the screen. Outside, a bird's voice was chinking against the bleached-azure sky with the kind of sound the tombstone maker over by the train depot makes with his chisel, when you hear him from far away. Scotty looked down the street and up the alley and into backyards, expecting to see Billy Bob Skaggs out there somewhere watching his house. If Billy Bob's dad had cut off a nigger man's ear, he knew, Billy Bob would do what he said he would do. While he was thinking about that a redbird landed in the dark waxy-green foliage of the grape arbor, stood there a moment bobbing his head, and then flew out and went out of sight over the house. Scotty could hear Link Bemis filing metal and singing over in his garage, husks of the sounds filtering up through the maples. The grass of the lawn below was intense green-gold and the maples made dim ponds of shade.

He had a spinning top. It was a metal disk on an axis, and when it was spun with the pull of a string, three little cog-edged, three-colored wheels would turn on the whirling disk and the top would blur to every imaginable color while the top whirred. He lay prone, running it on the rug instead of on the board floor so his mother wouldn't hear it. His chin was propped on his palms.

Whirling, changing from melon color to white, to yellow, the top crept toward the square of sunlight on the floor, humming. The dense dry must of the old rug was in his nose.

And then the top wandered into the sunlight and its color became a ghastly snot gray-green.

He had seen that color before. It was the color of the Huns' uniforms in a World War painting in the Encyclopedia. In the painting there had been a field as far as you could see covered with Huns wearing the snot-colored uniforms. In the foreground Hun soldiers with spikes on their helmets and bayoneted guns and dark mustaches were coming toward the Allies; the Allies were bleeding on the ground in tan suits behind sandbags and the Huns were coming forward looking out of dark soulless eyes like the eyes of the men in the barbershop. The top spun and kept the mustard-snot color, quivering, wobbling in the sunlight, and the smell of the dusty, musty battle came up out of the floor.

Suddenly, his body contracted violently twice and he threw up on the rug.

Rain was falling straight down. It was Friday. The swing creaked on its chains and the gray painted boards of the porch floor came and went, came and went, under it. His feet, sticking straight out before him, sailed forward, paused, went back. If he watched his feet, the floor blurred; if he watched the floor, his feet blurred.

His mother was writing on a tablet. She liked to write poems he couldn't quite understand but they were pretty to hear when she read them. After a while she stopped writing and just read, and after another while she stopped reading. Every few seconds she would push the floor with her foot to keep the swing going. He still had not told her about the cat, and they had not talked much for two days. It hurt to have her mad for so long.

Beyond the white-and-gray painted porch pillars and rails the maple limbs and barberry sprigs were dark from the rain and the street had flowing water on its bricks steaming with rain-spatters. The rain hissed noisily straight down everywhere beyond the porch. It poured from the downspouts into the mossy earth at the house corners with a crinkling sound. In the trees the rain hushed and on the lawn nearer by it hissed.

"Your father cut the Uncle Wiggily out of the Indianapolis papers and sent them down," she said. "Would you like to read them?" Maybe she was having a hard time not talking to him, too.

He shook his head and his Army cap went awry. He reached up with both hands and took the front and back peaks of it and straightened it.

"Do you like your new Army hat?"

"Yes, but it's an overseas cap, not a hat, remember?"

"Oh, yes. I'm sorry. Remember to thank your father for it."

"I will."

The swing went on awhile and the rain slowed and stopped. The swinging could make your stomach go woop sometimes but not make you sick as the top had the other day. But maybe thinking about the color of the top while you were swinging could. So he tried to keep from thinking about it, and about the Hun uniforms, and about the unknowable meanness in the eyes of men.

"Listen," his mother said. "There's the train whistle."

He listened and heard it way off, more like a short pressure on the air than a sound. The next time it was a sound. And after a while they could hear the distant engine, like a dog's panting.

By the time they could hear the train chuffing into the depot down by the river on the other side of town, the late afternoon sun had pried up the dark lid of clouds at the western horizon. It peeked in across the town and flooded the wet trees with gold and diamonds, and the clouds in the east looked purple beyond the leaves. The boy watched the weather change and tried not to think about the unresolved things. So he just looked and thought and nibbled inside his lips.

"Don't do that," she said.

"What?"

"With your lips."

"Mother?"

"Yes?"

"After it rains, it always looks like morning, doesn't it?"

She looked out at the sky. Then she looked at him, thoughtful.

"Yes," she said. "It does." She opened her tablet and wrote something quickly. Then, to herself: "I wonder why grownups can't see things that way."

"You can't?"

"Not until children tell us to look, we can't."

"Why not?"

"I don't know. But we can't."

"CAN not or MAY not?" he said, thinking of her little song.

She didn't answer, only sighed. She was no happier than he was about their trouble.

Across town the train's bell now was ringing. Faintly heard, the exhalation of steam and then the climbing shortening chuffing and the rattly jerking of the cars as it pulled them away from the depot.

The swing creaked. Now Scotty and his mother were watching toward the corner where Major Montgomery would appear soon around the brick side of the Bemis garage as he did every Friday evening.

"Mother," Scotty said timorously, "we don't have to tell Father about my haircut, do we?"

"But he'll see it. We'll have to tell him that Mr. Skaggs did it without permission."

"But it looks better to have my hair short with a—an overseas cap."

"M-hm. But I don't like what Mr. Skaggs did and I'm sure your father will want to talk to him."

He nibbled his lips some more and turned escapes and excuses over in his mind as fast as he could. He said:

"Couldn't we just tell him, uh, that I *asked* Mr. Skaggs to cut it short?" It seemed to him that he must bring it around to the truth before his father got home.

Her shoes hit the floor and the swing lurched to a stop. She was frowning, pointing a finger at him.

"Now, listen to me, young man. Don't you ever EVER tell a lie like that to your father, and don't ever ask me to help you tell him a lie!"

He blinked and swallowed and flushed. He was puzzled. Now when he wanted to tell the truth his mother was warning him not to because it would be a lie. To her it would be. It seemed it had to be right and wrong, either way.

"Here he comes," she said. "Now you *must* be truthful."

They met him on the sidewalk in front of the house. He knelt down and hugged Scotty, smelling his wonderful father-man smells of Neat's Foot Oil and soap and sweat and tobacco. He was very lean and his hands and face were as tan as his Sam Browne belt. On his collar was the little golden-cross chaplain's insignia. His copper-colored mustache was bristly against his son's cheek. His hat was off and his forehead was white, lightly freckled, below the short reddish hair that the boy had wanted his to look like.

The major straightened up and kissed his wife and she fussed that the neighbors would see, but she was happy. Then the major hoisted his son up and held him sitting on his forearm, and looked at him.

"Well, you're awfully quiet, Gimme-Gitme-Buyme. Aren't you going to ask me if I brought you anything?"

"Thank you for the overseas cap, Daddy."

"Ah, you're welcome! Now, there's some good manners."

"Did you?"

"Did I . . ."

"Get me anything?"

The major chuckled.

"I got you an overseas cap. And you look fine in it."

"But that was last week."

"So it was. And what have I done for you lately, hm? Well, let me see." He knelt on the sidewalk and fumbled with the button on the pocket below the ribbons on his tunic. He had ribbons because he had been in that war against the Huns. Scotty looked at the face of his father and saw again that it was not the kind of face the Huns had, or the men in the barbershop. There are two kinds of faces, the boy decided: like ours and like theirs.

"Here we are," said his father.

It was a narrow cardboard box and it was heavy. Inside was a tan stone with flat sides and straight edges.

"That's a whetstone to keep your pocketknife sharp. In a little bit I'll show you how to use it. You put oil on the stone and sharpen your knife as sharp as mine." He got his penknife out of his trouser pocket and opened it and demonstrated how it would shave hairs right off the veined brown wrist. The major was a very good woodcarver and when he had spare time he whittled whistles and ball-in-cages and funny-looking little caricatures of people in the town.

"Isn't he kind of young for a knife that sharp?"

"Oh, no, Grace. He's more likely to hurt himself with a dull knife than a sharp one."

"Thank you," Scotty said, thinking of the knife blade going back and forth on the stone, eager to learn how. "Could you show me now?"

"No," said his mother. "Your father's got to go down to talk to Mister Skaggs first, and then there are other things to discuss."

"Skaggs? The barber? What for?"

She reached, and the boy felt the cap being lifted off his head. His father looked at him with little wrinkles gathering at the corners of his gray eyes.

"I'll be blessed," he said, smiling. "Just like your father's, eh?" And then his smile went away as she told about Mrs. Franklin and the cat.

Half of the sky still had dark clouds but straight up was a billowing ragged edge white and orange with smears of slate color and the rest of the sky was very clear.

Drops fell like sparks from the maple leaves but were cool sparks leaving wet tiny cool spots where they fell on cloth or skin. Scotty and his father crossed the raindark pavement and went along the windowless wall of Bemis's Garage and turned the corner onto Main Street. Holding on to his father's hand, he tried to step around the puddles on the sidewalk. Their feet smacked on the wet concrete. There were beads of water on his father's shiny Army shoes. His big hands had bluish veins and reddish hair and wrinkles on their knuckles.

They came to the empty lot. The hollyhocks were bowed and dripping. The boy was reluctant and full of dark foreboding.

The major stopped suddenly in front of Hendricks's Grocery.

"Look up there," he said.

Beyond the other end of town, there was a double rainbow, one arc perfectly within the other.

"You don't see a double one very often," said the major, who liked rainbows. Once he had given Scotty an Army shoulder insignia that was a rainbow of shiny colored threads and the boy now had it on one of his coats, the rainbow that his father had worn when he was in the World War with the Huns. He had killed Huns in the war and that had changed him and he had become a preacher and chaplain.

They stood in front of the store looking at the double rainbow against the purple storm clouds in the east. The windows of Stillabower's Drug Store blazed bright orange with the reflection of the sunset. There was a wet fresh grassy sweet smell. The two black cars parked on the Main Street, one by the Moose Lodge and the other by the hardware store, were very smooth and shiny black with blue beads of water on them.

"Will there be Huns in the new war?" Scotty asked.

His father's knees cracked softly as he knelt.

"How do you know there's going to be a new war?"

"Once you told Mother there always are."

"Yes." His father's eyes were crinkled at the edges and he looked past the end of the street and past the double rainbow. "And there will be Huns," he said. "But they call them Germans now. Nazis."

"Mother calls me Hun sometimes."

"No," the major said, smiling. "She calls you Hon H-O-N for Honey, instead of H-U-N for German."

"Daddy?"

"Yes?"

"You don't really want to talk to Mister Skaggs, do you?"

"Well, not especially. But your mother's right; I ought to. He shouldn't't've done that without permission."

The boy's knees were shaking. "What if I told him to?"

"Your mother said you didn't, though."

"Well, but. I might of."

"Might have? What do you mean, you might have?"

The boy answered nothing. He compressed his lips and looked away from his father's face.

"Come on, now. Did you tell the barber to?"

"I forget."

"Are you telling me a lie? Did you tell your mother a lie? Look at me and answer."

His father's face was very close and there were two sharp wrinkles up and down between his red eyebrows. For an instant the face seemed to be flat and cold like a picture, or—he felt a chilling fright— like the faces in the barbershop, the OTHER kind of faces instead of OUR kind.

"Why do you keep looking away from me? Now look here and tell me the truth or I'm going to have to punish you." Waiting for the answer, the major shifted his kneeling weight to the ball of his right foot from his left. His forearms rested on his knees; his hands were bent down at the wrists and the long fingers of his right hand were loosely closed over the fingers of the left. The boy looked into the gray eyes, which were still watching levelly and waiting.

"I told him to make mine like yours."

A change passed through the major's face, an instant's tenderness that made it close and familiar again; but almost immediately he narrowed his lips again and the lines reappeared between the brows.

"Well, then, Mister Skaggs didn't do anything wrong, then, did he?"

"No, sir."

"And we shouldn't go down to his house and admonish him, should we?"

"What's admonish?"

"We shouldn't say anything unpleasant to him."

"No."

The major reached up and pulled his earlobe. He was still frowning.

"Do you know what the worst thing is, about the lie you told? You tried to put the blame on somebody else instead of yourself, didn't you?"

"I guess."

"What do you mean, you guess?"

"I mean, yes, sir, I did."

"You see, you don't ever have to *guess* you've done something wrong. You know. Don't you?"

"Yes, sir," he said, before realizing that even that was not true.

"Were you afraid I wouldn't want you to have a haircut like mine?"

"No. I was afraid because I didn't ask Mother first."

"All right, I think we can clear that little matter up well enough. If you'd just told your mother the truth right at first, you wouldn't have had all this trouble. Can you see that?"

"Yes, sir."

"So now we have this matter of you torturing a cat." He drew his fingers down his long jaw. "That's a much more serious thing, and I pray to God that you can satisfy me as well on that. So tell me about it. And I *won't* abide another lie."

Scotty felt a rush of yearning. He wanted to tell his father about Billy Bob, wanted to so badly he felt like crying. Surely if he told the truth about it, his father wouldn't let Billy Bob hurt him.

But the major was only home on weekends. Every Saturday evening he got on the train and went away to Fort Harrison at Indianapolis and was gone until the next Friday.

I'll cut your ear off, Billy Bob had said.

"Daddy, I promise. I didn't do anything to the cat."

"Ah-ah!" the major cautioned, head tilting, eyes hardening again.

"It's the truth! Cross my heart!"

"Scotty, I'm so ashamed of you I don't know what to say!"

"It's truuue!" He began to shake with sobs now.

"I'm a man of God," his father declared, standing up away from Scotty, "and I don't like corporal punishment. But you *will* honor your father and mother and that means you will tell us the truth!" He grabbed Scotty by the wrist in a painful grasp. "I give you one more chance to admit what you did, and if you don't, I have to take you home and lay the belt on you! Scotty, for Heaven's sake, I don't want to hurt my own flesh and blood, my only son! But I swear, you'll admit what you've done or your bottom's going to have more stripes on it than a top sergeant!"

"All right! All right!" Scotty cried out. "I did it! I wanted . . . I wanted . . . I was just trying to scare the cat!" he lied. "I did it and now please leave me alone!" He was crumbling inside.

The major sucked in the corner of his mouth, sighed, and looked off toward the end of the street. Scotty looked, too, and the rainbows were gone. The big hand came down on his shoulder and made him turn around on the sidewalk, toward home.

The sun was behind the big trees as they walked homeward. Its light flickered through the leaves into their eyes. Ahead there were pools and splashes and puddles of wet sunlight on the street and sidewalk. They walked and squinted at the sunlight that seemed to flash from everywhere. The boy didn't notice that his father was looking down at him as they walked, looking down with worries and sadness in his eyes.

For his confessed cruelty to a dumb animal, Scotty was denied his Friday-night supper and was sent to his room. The matter had made it harder than ever to know what is right and what is wrong. But that night as the sun went down outside his bedroom window he decided that he could no longer honor his father or his mother.

Not if they could believe he would hurt a kitty.

They were downstairs in the library. Their voices drifted vaguely up into his bedroom where he sat on the edge of his bed in pajamas, making a decision.

He got up and took off the pajamas and hung them on the knob of the bedpost. He pulled on his corduroy long pants and a sweatshirt, and his tennis shoes. Then he took his school-book satchel out of the drawer and unloaded the books and pencils and tablet onto the dresser. He put his whetstone into the case, and his knife. Then he crept into the bathroom and got a towel, his toothbrush, and a can of tooth powder, carried them back to his room, and put them in the satchel. Then he put in the overseas cap. He remembered the jacket with the rainbow shoulder patch and got it out of the closet and put it on the bed to take. He looked about here and there in the half light of the room. His chin was trembling but he was determined not to cry. Finally he put a pencil and a paper tablet back in the satchel and folded it shut and buckled it.

That's all I need, he thought. I have a dollar. I can get out now if I don't make much noise on the stairs. I better not let them see me or they'll beg me not to go and I'll have to not cry or smile and say, I'm going, you can't stop me, and I don't want them to cry or get mad.

I wish I could take Laddie but he'd bark and give me away.

I'm glad the moon is out. I can see by it to walk even if I go out past the streetlights.

I hope Mother and Father don't worry and stay awake all night thinking about me out past the streetlights. I don't honor them but I don't want them to feel bad.

I better take a blanket too because the moon doesn't make you warm like the sun because it isn't made out of fire and it just looks shiny because of the sun on it, Daddy says.

That's funny.

"Hon, is that you?" his mother's voice came through the library door. She had heard the stair-step squeak. The boy opened his mouth to answer. But he was at the bottom of the stairs now and knew he couldn't be seen from the library door. So he stood still and did not answer. His heart beat strongly and he waited tight-poised to see if she was going to come out into the hall.

"He's in bed, isn't he?" his father's voice asked beyond the library door.

"Yes," she replied. "I just thought I heard something on the steps."

"It's just this old house settling." Then there was a yawn and the deep voice went on: "But this is a good old place. If I could find a place like this up at Indianapolis I'd have you come up there to live. Then I could come in from the fort every night, and not be just a weekend father."

"Or weekend husband?"

He laughed softly. "But you just can't find a house like this up there. At least not that we could afford on Army pay."

While they're talking they can't hear me open the screen door, the boy thought. I better go now. Right there there's a place there where the porch floor squeaks so I better step here.

"Listen, darling," his mother's voice said. He froze again. But she said, "When he was out roaming one day it gave me an idea for a poem. . . ."

Outside the screen door the night was cool black and full of the creaking and croaking of crickets and frogs. He looked anxiously out and saw the long deep shadows of the maple trunks and the green halo of leaves around the streetlamp. Something urged him to go back upstairs, or stop and listen to what his mother had written about him. He was sleepy and the darkness outside did not look comforting, but he had decided. So he put his hand against the screen doorframe and pushed slowly. The door spring thrummed and groaned rustily on its hook. He stepped out onto the welcome mat on the porch. Leaf shadows moved slightly in the weak glow of the streetlight. He could still hear his mother's voice inside the house. He eased the door shut and crept down onto the sidewalk. He turned and looked at the library window and saw the bun on the back of his mother's head glossy under the reading lamp.

"Let me fix a line here," her voice said, then dropped.

He turned left and began to walk northward.

He heard Laddie say "burf" in his deep voice out in his doghouse, and prayed to God that he would not start barking out. The prayer worked and Laddie made no more sound. Now the boy crossed the street and watched his shadow come out from under him on the street and stretch out before him into the black tunnel under trees ahead. He came to the shaded part of the sidewalk and walked in. As soon as he was out of the light of the streetlamp he trembled, and stopped to look back at the house. Like a long clawing black hand, the shadow of a maple limb sprawled across the moon-white boards, and distantly, heat lightning flared. He wondered if Billy Bob Skaggs was out there in the dark.

The Night Coach to Bloomington

Lee Zacharias

R. SCHUNK died on the Tuesday of my music theory final my first semester at Indiana University. It was a day as dreary as the Friday, earlier in the semester, when John F. Kennedy was killed and I had sloshed to the Music Building to give the other members of the I.U. Philharmonic the news. It had been raining ever since, a wall of dirty clouds the apparent portal to Heaven.

Mr. Schunk had never moved to Arizona, though every Wednesday and Saturday until I left for college I listened to him mourn his coming exile. He saw hardly anything save the milk of his cataracts, and when he grew temperamental, thumping a knotted finger against the music stand for sharps I had not missed, calling crescendos where there were none, my own temper rose. Yet for me he was the perfect maestro, with an ear so cantankerous that I learned to trust my own. Another teacher might have taught me to count more accurately, to play as I was told; he taught me to *imagine* the music, as passionately as if I had written it myself. I was the first freshman ever seated in the I.U. Philharmonic, but more than once in rehearsal the conductor glared me down to say, "Miss Hurdle, may I remind you that there is an orchestra playing with you?" More than once the conductor of the

65

Richmond Symphony had to do the same. When Howard Feltner, my clarinet teacher at Indiana, first heard me play, he said, "You've got a lot of style, and your tempo is eccentric but good, but you're too loud in the fortes and too soft in the pianissimos. Now I'm going to mark this up, and I want you to do it my way." I put down my Paris Selmer. From it I had coaxed a tone that ranged from the dark hues of the German to the brittle, chromatic tints of the French. "I won't," I said and thought of Mr. Schunk. "You're blind as a bat," I'd said to him once. "You can't even read the notes." Mr. Schunk squared his shoulders. "When the eye cannot see, the ear can hear. And when the ear is deaf, the heart will know." I picked up the clarinet and played the piece again, not exactly Feltner's way, but different, an improvement on my own.

But when the heart stops beating? Mr. Schunk's daughter called me. Her husband taught trumpet at Indiana, and from the day I'd arrived the Solomons had taken me in. She said, "Jane, I thought you'd want to know that my father passed away in his sleep this morning." She grunted. "Listen to me. We haven't even seen those funeral parasites yet, and already I'm speaking their language."

"Oh, Ruth." I gasped, shocked because Mr. Schunk rose for me in that moment in a way that, living, he had not been able to do all fall. I hadn't written; over Christmas I'd found some excuse not to visit. Our temperaments had battled for so long that I was afraid he hated me, and I didn't want to admit I'd needed him. I heard him saying, "When I come to America, I speak English. When I am at the ball park, I speak baseball. When I am playing music, I speak Italian." Now he was dead, and his daughter was speaking mortician.

"Now, Jane, don't be weepy. He didn't suffer."

I sniffed back my tears. "He was always suffering."

"Isn't that the truth?" Though I hadn't meant to be funny, Ruth laughed. "Martin and I are driving to Hammond this afternoon. Sam and Jake will probably thumb up from Champaign. I've told them they'll be lucky not to be killed. 'You know what kind of people pick up hitchhikers,' I said. 'Your beautiful young bodies will be shot full of holes and tossed out in a ditch.' But they never listen to me. David doesn't know—he didn't come home last night. You know how he is when he's got his thing up a new skirt. Anyway, we'll have plenty of room if you want to come along."

"Good Lord," I said.

"I'm just being realistic." Big-boned like her father, Ruth too was an epic complainer, though no one took her grievances as seriously as I had once taken his. Her voice was brusque, and she had a brisk way of walking, as if life were nothing two rolled sleeves and a bottle of ammonia couldn't cure. She was proud of her boys' bodies because she refused to admit she was proud of them, and I never heard her say a sentimental word about any of her sons, three grown and the two under five who had slipped through a hole in her diaphragm, she claimed. "There's nothing more ridiculous than an old woman with a baby," she would say as she slung diapers from the kitchen counter to fix a martini. She was still nursing Michael, and she often stirred the pitcher with one enormous tit hanging out. They lived in a big, sloppy frame house filled with tattered wicker, Oriental rugs, cats, dying plants, students, and noise. "I can't keep up—I'm not Superman," Ruth was moaning when I first punched the doorbell that was as defunct as her father's, having been invited for dinner my first Sunday in Bloomington at his suggestion. She glared at a basket of philodendron with brown leaves folded and clinging like dead moths to the stems. Two of Martin's pupils were already sitting on a willow settee, and, in spite of her, we politely praised Ruth's plants, her cheese dip, her cats, and her kids. She brightened. Michael was a regular monkey in motor skills, and Joshua, her fourth-born, would have a big dong. "I swear the kid's an idiot," she said, "but he's hung." We smiled nervously in search of something neuter to praise. "Well," she pursued, "it certainly can't hurt him." It didn't take me long to understand that her complaints were really declarations of love.

"Well," she said now, "do you want a ride or not?"

"Of course," I said, and so I went home.

I hadn't planned to, though my finals were over and there were almost two weeks of empty days before second semester began. No, I had decided, when the bus taking me home for Christmas crossed the Kankakee River into the cocoon of soot spun by the mills, home was where the heart beat wings against the wall. The week before the

Christmas recess, Dick lost his right index finger on a coil in the sheetmill. A wad of oozing gauze and adhesive tape hung from his hand. "My fault." He shrugged. "The mill's no place to be horsing around. You turn your back on those machines, you're lucky they don't cut you in half." We had Christmas dinner at his kitchen table, and he joked while I averted my eyes from the hand by his plate. "Never thought a fellow wore his nuts on his hand, but here I sit like a girl while my wife carves the turkey. What'll it be, Janie, light meat or dark?"

"I'm not hungry," I said. Dickie spilled his milk on my plate and made a pink swamp of my cranberry sauce. In the living room the television babbled; all morning the battery-run forklift my mother gave Dickie had lifted and lowered and lifted and whined. Everything depressed me: Marie's melon belly ripening under her maternity smock, new curtains, old platitudes, arguments, advice.

My mother wanted to know about my life, but dorm stories and gush about my classes bored her. She'd never had a roommate; she'd never taken theory. She had only worked in a cafeteria and got married. Oh, it wasn't that I didn't love them, though I wished they could talk about something besides labor pains and union dues; wished that my mother would remember I spent my time in the music library, not the *liberry*—I hadn't followed in her footsteps, and I didn't ring up fruit. "Well, what do you do if you don't go out?" she asked, and I told her about the Solomons. She frowned through my re-enactment of a particularly hilarious turn from our Sunday night charades, not waiting for the answer before she mused, "You know, your brother makes good money if they can just settle without a strike."

"I can't talk to you," I said. She shrugged. "I don't know why not. I never change." I packed for the few remaining weeks of first semester and explained I'd have to stay in Bloomington for break because the Phil was getting ready for a concert. "Suit yourself," she said.

At the bus station, which wore a tinsel garland above the ticket desk, Dick pinched my cheek with his left hand. "Don't be sad, Sissy." I stared at the rag claw he hadn't raised to touch me. He'd driven me to the station, and now I had to take leave of him alone. "Aw, come on, it isn't like I play the clarinet. For a man with a family, better a finger than your paycheck." I kept my eyes on his hand because I couldn't bear to look at his eyes. "I got a real family now."

"So, everyone's got family." I swooped to straighten the I.D. tag on my suitcase. "It's the universal misfortune."

"Hey." He stooped into an awkward hug. My mother usually shamed me into grudging manners; I treated him worse and loved him more because he never pouted, never ever shamed. "You calling me a misfortune? You're my family too."

"Well." I straightened. Why did I always want to hurt him? "Better your pay than a finger when it's time to diddle your wife."

He blushed. "Janie, those kind of things are private."

I grinned, but when he looked away, I was ashamed. "I didn't mean it. I was just *kidding.*" My bus had pulled into the shed. He picked up my suitcase. "I'm sorry, I'm sorry," I begged, clutching at his sleeve as we moved forward in the crush of passengers. I wanted to say something and did not know what it was.

He patted my shoulder. "Well, kid, don't take any wooden nickels." It was the goodbye my father had always used, and it sounded as stupid as it always had.

I looked up. The golden wings of the Presley pompadour stretched beyond his temples in a parody of flight. College boys wore short hair. The edge of his eyetooth was dark with rot. "I'm not coming back." So that was what I wanted to say. "I hate it here. Next summer I'm going to Chautauqua or someplace and get a job." He had the most beautiful, clean gray eyes, but the color now reminded me of lead. I grabbed his coat and pressed my face to the wool. "I don't hate you, I don't hate you, you're the only one I'll never hate."

"Course not." He raised my head and took the ticket from my hand. "Hey, you gotta get on the bus now. Take it easy. Why, when you get back to that college and start thinking about your good-looking brother, I bet you won't be able to wait to come home." The line of passengers was sidestepping us. "Besides, you can't tell me I went to all this trouble to make you an aunt again and you aren't even going to come see my kid." I stopped sniffling, and he bent to peck me.

As soon as I got to my seat, I opened my window. "Dick," I yelled, leaning into the damp, exhaust-fouled chill of the shed. He paused at the door to the station. "Write me a letter, okay? The only one who writes is Mom."

He smiled the saddest smile I've ever seen and held up his maimed right hand in reply. And I meant that to be my last memory of Hammond. But then Mr. Schunk died.

My mother was surprised to see me. It was her day off, and she was lounging on the sofa in a pink duster while a soap man threatened to leave his soap wife on TV. "I don't know why I watch," she apologized, flicking off the set. "Nothing ever happens." She put the coffeepot on, and we sat at the kitchen table. It was hard for me to believe that she was only four years older than Ruth, though her dark hair was just beginning to gray and Ruth's was steel-colored, pulled back into an untidy scouring-pad bun. Ruth would go slack-faced like her father; already her flesh had begun to sag. Save for a little crêpe under the eyes, my mother's had held tight for forty-nine years.

But Ruth was my friend, and my mother was my mother, and if she gave the same advice as my mother, at least Ruth gave it from the gut. And Ruth practiced what she preached, while my mother, nine years after my father died, still listed our phone in his name. In the car on the way up, Ruth lamented that her father had never remarried. "Life goes on," she said. "You may as well make up your mind to go with it, and it's a shame to die alone. That's just the way I feel." She'd been disgusted when she heard that I didn't date. "Now, you listen to me, Jane Hurdle. You're only a freshman, and already you've got a good reputation at the school. But music isn't everything. We didn't get those five kids with a trumpet."

I was willing to admit that Ruth had a point. So I'd had a bad experience when I was twelve—tough luck. I had used it as an excuse much too long. I wasn't twelve anymore, and it was no longer sex that put me off: it was hangnails, pimples, and bald spots on the grad students. The men I knew were brilliant but guilty of dead skin, pustules, or thinning hair.

And so, throughout first semester I was lonely when the dorm emptied on Saturday nights. Their faces knocked cockeyed, their blouses buttoned wrong, the girls in the hall jammed the elevator at 1:00 A.M., squealing and sighing. They *said* they were virgins, but I knew better. Sandy Gitzke had tipped me off: everyone did it, no matter what she said. A cute Beta in my comp class invited me to his pledge dance. I wanted to go, but I was embarrassed to tell him I couldn't do the leg, the mashed potatoes, or even the twist. Instead, I told him I didn't date. "Not ever?" He looked startled. "Not ever," I said. He had a beautiful blond bang and a stomach as lean and hard as a washboard. I imagined us in a dark room, Brahms on the stereo while that soft blond hair brushed my breast. But he didn't listen to Brahms, and I didn't dance. Sidney, my roommate, spent the nights between dances in the television room of the Lambda Chi house, where the only light was the gray snow of the screen, and the windows were painted black so that Lambda Chis could drink and screw their girlfriends in private. While she was out, I stood on a chair and looked myself over in the mirror. I'd barely hit five feet, but I had high, round tits like whole notes in my pockets. From hip to waist and back, I was a harmonic minor, ascending and descending. I was ready, but only if I could find someone as beautiful as that Beta willing to sit out the dances with me. I let Sidney fix me up.

His name was Eddie Ziegler, and he was drunk when he got there. While he crawled under coffee tables with a foot of garden hose, whining, "Friend or enema?," I spent the evening watching "Gunsmoke" with Sidney and her boyfriend. On the way home he snatched my wrap-around skirt and charged a Volkswagen on Third Street, screaming, "El toro, el fucking toro, mother," leaving me on the curb, sobbing and shivering in my lace-trimmed pettipants. I forgave Sidney, who swore it wasn't her fault and Eddie could be a riot when he wasn't stinko, but I didn't let her fix me up again.

Should I have explained all that to my mother as we sat at the kitchen table, drinking coffee, and she said, "When you said you were staying at school, I hoped it was maybe because you'd met somebody"?

Not on your life. Ruth had roared when I described my date with Eddie. My mother would have used it to teach me a lesson. What kind of friends was I making at that college? She wanted me to have a good time, but only on her terms.

She twisted her wedding ring and stared at her coffee. "How can you see with all that hair in your eyes?" I ducked my head as she reached to smooth back my bangs. "Well, I should of known you wouldn't bother to come home to see me. I suppose I ought to be glad you came home at all."

"That's a crummy thing to say."

"I didn't *mean* I was glad about Mr. Schunk. Although . . ." She had this way of beginning sentences with *thoughs,* as if everything she said had been preceded by a point she took exception to. "You have to look at it this way, Janie. His family must be relieved he went so fast." She shook her head. "You were too young to remember. It's terrible when they linger like your father." She looked out the window for a minute. "Ever since you went to college, we're not good enough for you."

"That's not so," I said, hating her for bringing it up and hating myself because, of course, it was true.

The light that came through the window behind her was gray. We hadn't turned on the fluorescent light—no sense in wasting electricity in the afternoon. The dim room was a memorial to my father's tight-fisted ghost. "I feel like I'm onstage," he had said once, when he came into my bedroom and found me, under overhead and Cinderella lamp, reading *The Bobbsey Twins and Baby May*. When he snapped off that silly dresser lamp, I stood on my bed and pummeled the front of his gray work shirt with my fists. "I'm reading," I shrieked. "My teacher says you have to have good light when you read." He'd shrugged me off. "Your teacher don't pay the bills." He died less than two years later, a gray man in work shoes and twills who'd allotted our lives in kilowatt hours. Now my mother's face was dreary with shadow. She rubbed a finger in a coffee stain till nothing was left but a wavy brown ring and her iridescent print. My heart constricted with family: my brother, those little evasive rubs. I jerked my hands from the table.

"Well, they say you always hurt the ones you love."

"Will you drop it?" Oh Lord, would I never be done with that noose they call kin? Why couldn't my mother, like Ruth, complain in an epic tradition? Why did she always bring up the tedious, small business of love? "I'm sorry if I hurt your feelings, but would you please, *please* just get to the point?"

"Never mind," she said in a voice as worn as the rubber heels on my loafers. "You're not interested." She took another sip of coffee. "Oh, honey, I *am* glad to see you. It's just that I worry about you, working so hard. Don't you ever feel like getting out?"

"You don't go out," I said.

"Me?" She looked surprised. "I'm an old grandmother."

"But you don't look like a grandmother, and you're prettier than Sidney's mother or Ruth, and they're not even as old as you."

She smiled and covered my hand with hers. Like mine, her fingernails were ragged. Weak nails, nice legs, a stubborn habit of solitude—they ran in the family, so what did she expect? "Do you think so? Why, Janie." I don't think I ever saw her look so pleased.

"Besides," I growled, embarrassed, "I tried to get out over Christmas. I wanted to go to the Chicago Symphony, but you didn't want me riding the South Shore that late, and Dick wouldn't take me because Marie had to go to some dumb shower."

"That shower meant a lot to her. After all, being a mother is the most important job in the world." My mother rose and dashed the dregs of her coffee into the sink. "You know yourself those trains don't run very often at night. Anyway, I didn't mean with your brother."

The phone rang.

She sighed. "Well, maybe you do get out and just don't tell me. You always were secretive."

"I'm not secretive."

"Answer the phone," she said. "You're closer."

It was Dickie. "Is my mom there?" he asked. "Who's this? Grandma?"

"It's Jane," I said.

"Aunt Jane," he whooped. "What a pickle." That was the advertising slogan for Aunt Jane's Polish Dills, and whenever I was crabby, he called me Aunt Dill. "Let me talk to Grandma."

So my mother forgot about my social life and hung up in a snit because Marie was missing. She had disappeared, it turned out, all the way next door, but my mother didn't feel the least bit foolish, because, as she said, "when a woman is due any minute, you want to know where she is." When I pointed out that she wasn't due for another three weeks, my mother added that I didn't know anything—the baby could decide to come any day.

And even though it would prove her right, I halfway hoped it would. After all, I would be its aunt. And something had to pass the time.

I saw the Solomons only at Mr. Schunk's funeral, which wasn't at the synagogue. Though the Solomons weren't observant, immediately after the burial, they honored Mr. Schunk his way by starting the traditional mourning period, staying at the house I had visited so often. There they received the rabbi and members of the congregation who came to say the prayer for the dead, as well as Dick and Marie and me, but all we did was sit. Hadn't I reminded Mr. Schunk of a daughter? But his daughter just sat, too. I wasn't so sure that was his way. He'd told me himself that he was a musician first and second a Jew. Martin and I were also musicians, but at the funeral all we could do was listen to some boring old man eulogize the goodness of the departed without mentioning the Chicago Symphony, while the vibrato of that good-ness—those first notes of Stravinsky—rippled up and down my spine. Believing in nothing, I felt like nothing, too. The Jews said they were God's chosen people. So did Catholics, and my brother had turned Catholic when he married Marie. Everyone I knew seemed to be headed for a heaven where I would not be welcome. I banged my heel against the leg of my folding chair. If God existed, I didn't like him. Mr. Schunk had been an artist. What could he want with that pretentious mediocrity Yahweh, the old jaw-well, who kept time in a tedium of hour upon twenty-four hours while musicians worked with what was given and created counter-rhythm? Given a choice of life or art, I could not understand who would think life the superior invention.

I didn't see much of my brother either. He was working double shifts to put aside something extra in case he went out on strike that spring. His hand had healed, the bandage replaced by an angry stub of red flesh that would later whiten. He had transferred from the sheetmill back to open hearth. Mostly he talked baby, patting Marie's barrel of a belly.

Dickie took me to his room to show me the squeak-toy, a blue rubber baseball mitt he'd bought with his very own money to present to his new brother. "But, Dickie," I protested, even though at seven he was already insisting his name was Rick, "what if your new brother is a sister?" He widened the brown eyes he'd got from his mother. "Aunt Dill, if it's a girl, she won't be my brother, and if I don't get a brother, I'm going to give my *present*"—he said the word contemptuously, as if I'd tainted it—"to the orphans." "Don't you like girls?" I asked. He grinned. "Aunt Jane, would you loan me five dollars? 'Cause with five dollars I can buy a real one, and if I don't get a brother I can use it myself." "Dickie," I said sternly, "it's the thought that counts." He frowned. "But Aunt Jane, if I get a baseball glove, I won't care if I don't get a brother." How's that for thought? I gave him five dollars because I thought, never mind his mother's eyes, the little bastard takes after me.

But my generosity didn't buy me a baby, though, to prove my mother right, it did come early, choosing the day I was scheduled to leave. So, with my suitcase and a shopping bag full of books and scores in one hand and in the other the $700 Paris Selmer, which I had spent evenings after school and two summers spooning dead goldfish from a tank in the basement of W. T. Grant's to earn, I struggled up the steps of a city bus to get to the Greyhound station downtown. The Solomons were staying an extra day, doing whatever you did to begin settling an estate—call Goodwill, for all I knew, to haul away the rickety furniture and fans that were Mr. Schunk's wealth.

You wouldn't have caught my roommate on a city bus or a Greyhound either. Sidney had her own car, a 1962 Rambler she parked illegally behind the Lambda Chi house because freshmen weren't allowed to have wheels. Yesterday afternoon she would have driven from Greensburg to Bloomington to check her mailbox for sorority bids. She wouldn't move to the house till next fall, but all spring, I knew, she'd be busy with pledge dinners and mixers. Besides Ruth, she was my only real friend, and I felt I was losing her. "Another dinner with the big shots?" Sid had teased as I dressed for one of my evenings at the Solomons'. I shrugged. At the Music School, I hinted, all the students fraternized with profs, but in fact freshmen usually didn't. I was different: honors and in the Phil, almost a member of the Solomon family. Having nowhere else to go, I was grateful, though I sometimes felt like a mascot in my knee socks and pleated skirts. Still, I beat my piano teacher at charades; the grad students listened to my opinions. And, while I was short on experience, I was long on opinions. Martin was nice, though his idea of sparking conversation was to ask what you thought of your classes or the Cubs. He blushed at anything off-color, and, though he laughed when I thunked his head to act out "Night on Bald Mountain," he turned purple when I pantomimed "mount." If Ruth hadn't been there to direct him, I suspected he might have indeed tried to beget his get with a trumpet.

So what if I had my dinners? Without Sidney I would have no one to giggle with, and show me a girl who doesn't like to giggle, I'll show you a girl who is a freak. "There's nothing wrong with Janie," I'd overheard Dick insist to my mother. "She's just special." I was more hurt than mad to hear her reply, "Maybe that's her problem." Sidney made me feel normal. She borrowed my shampoo; she asked my advice as if boyfriends were something I would know about. Together we bitched about mystery-meat meals and after hours let down a basket on a rope for pizza. But next year she wouldn't be in our blue room on the third floor of the limestone castle that looked like a medieval fortress with real ivory towers. Of course, I might not either. We had heard rumors that Morrison would be converted to a class-room building, and any leftover maidens who didn't graduate or pledge or get married would be shipped off to the newer dorms on the fringes of campus.

But even a new dorm would be better than the sooty air of Hammond, which I was leaving like last year's skin, and I thought how glad I was to be going back as I walked the dead length of State Street to the bus station, past Goodwill and toward the burned-out strip of Calumet City, where a poster in front of a boarded-up burlesque invited you in to see Lottie the Fabulous Body, whose legs flapped in wet paper shreds from her fabulous hips. It was snowing, and tire treads cut through the street like pastry wheels, but the sky looked as if it had been rolled out of a tandem mill. In the station I slumped in a chair and picked enamel flakes from the painted canvas seat. I watch-ed a student who sat on a plaid suitcase chatter with her girlfriend, whose Weejuns dripped dirty puddles around her feet. The girl with the Weejuns lived in Morrison; I'd seen her in the lobby. I supposed there was a bid waiting in her mailbox or maybe a proposal from a distant boyfriend. Behind them a Negro woman with a belly the size of Marie's slapped at a knock-kneed little girl, who screamed, "I be good, I be good. Just don't hit me again, nigger." In the alcove that had once been a concession stand, its dusty shelves now empty, the cash register flagged no-sale, drawer distended like an idiot mouth, a girl was weeping on her boyfriend's shoulder. Next to me a hand belonging to an old man who reeked of wool and perspiration throbbed beneath a newspaper. The bus would stop in Kentland and Lafayette before I changed coaches in Indianapolis (why, oh why, do they call them coaches?) to pick up a fresh supply of perverts, derelicts, and ex-cons. I got up to get a cup of coffee.

I'd been wrong about the failure of metamorphoses in Hammond; they happened every day, even if they happened backward. In the terminal restaurant I saw a man become a dog.

The waitress's powdered face had the texture of sandstone, and two glittering black eyes peered through clean little holes under painted-on brows. When Sidney asked what my father did, I'd been relieved to tell her my father was dead. Her father was a doctor. When her parents visited, they took us to the Fireside for lobster Newburg. The waiters wore red jackets and bow ties. I wouldn't have wanted to confess that my father had shoveled coal in a mill or that, when you ate on us, you went to Fat Boy's, where my sister-in-law, who wore a big button that said TRY OUR FRESH STRAWBERRY PIE, instead of a Kappa key or Pi Phi arrow, had wiped tables.

At the counter a man in an oversized gray loden coat trailing threads of lining ordered water and handed her the menu. Her eye holes slit, and he cackled. She folded her arms and watched until his laughter shook him loose and he clutched at the counter, fingers slipping over the edge and disappearing into the crumple of his coat as the stool toppled and rang. She picked up a rag and began polishing the counter. "Bitch," he yelled, rearing his head from the tatters. He began crawling, tangling arms and legs in the coat before her wadded rag hit his neck and his limbs buckled. I stood, no longer thirsty. He threw his head back again. "I ain't dirt . . . can't treat me . . . call my lawyer . . ." As she howled with laughter, he bayed at a peel of paint hanging from the tin ceiling, then lunged at the wet hem of my slacks and barked up my leg.

"Stop it," I begged, scooping up my books and thumping my suitcase. "Go away."

He bit my ankle. The waitress was bleating with laughter. For a moment I simply did not believe it. There was no rocket of pain through the corduroy and sweat sock. Nevertheless the son-of-a-bitch had sunk his teeth in my pant leg.

"Your lawyer, my ass," the waitress hollered, bowing her head to the counter and wiping her eyes. "What you need is a rabies shot."

"Lady, I need a dime." I shook my foot, and he fell back.

"Aw, go on, get out of here before I sweep you up with the trash," the waitress said.

He raised his head. "Lady, I ain't askin' for the Purple Heart, just a thin silver medallion." He rose to his knees and clasped one of mine. "You don't even have to hang it on a ribbon. Just 'In God we trust' and, when you turn it over, 'E pluribus unum.' A dime, lady. You gotta have a medal to make a fuckin' phone call." He howled a crescendo, throwing himself forward so hard, his chin cracked on the tile.

"He's dead," I guessed, looking up at the stony bluff of the waitress's face.

"I should be so lucky." She sat across from me and put her hands on the table, her fingers smelling faintly of disinfectant. "The jackass comes in once a week and writes filth on the menus, but this is the first time I ever seen him bite a customer."

I struggled upstairs to the ladies' room and dredged my purse for a dime. I didn't have one, and the free stall was filled with mops, buckets, and spare rolls. No wonder the hall stank of urine. When the two girls from downstairs came in, I waited for one to finish so that I could sneak in without paying. "Look at it this way," Plaid Suitcase called to the Weejuns. "If you don't get your B.A., you'll get your M.R.S." They laughed. I pulled up my pant leg and peeked down my sock, disappointed that there was no mark on my ankle, something to prove Hammond to Sid. When they flushed, I jumped for a door. In case you've never noticed, only middle-aged women pass on pay toilets.

By the time I clumped downstairs, the loudspeaker was gargling my bus call. The station had jammed with people in a hurry to leave Hammond, and I was lucky to get a place by the window. There was nothing I wanted to see, but I spread my luggage and tried to look mean in hopes of hogging the seat. Just as the bus began wheezing and revving, the girl who had wept on her boyfriend's shoulder puffed down the aisle, sniffling while I took back my clarinet and shopping bag to let her sit. She leaned across my lap and beat on the window, waving to the boy, who grew smaller in the shed as we pulled into

State Street. She sobbed all the way to Kentland. In the parking lot of the Post House she looked up. "I won't see him till February." She whimpered, her swollen face working. "And what if he meets somebody?" "Oh damnit," I said, "turn off that faucet," and she sniveled into her coat sleeve all the way to Indianapolis, where I caught the night coach to Bloomington.

Can I Just Sit Here for a While?

Ron Hansen

H E WAS called a traveler and that was another thing he loved about the job. If you wanted the hairy truth, Rick Bozack couldn't put his finger on any one thing that made the job such a clincher; it might have been his expense account or the showroom smell of his leased Oldsmobile or the motel rooms: God, the motel rooms, twin double beds and a stainless steel Kleenex dispenser and a bolted-down color TV topped with cellophane-wrapped peppermints which the maid left after she cleaned. He loved the thermos coffee canister the waitress banged down on his table at breakfast, he loved the sweat on his ice-water glass, he loved the spill stains blotting through the turned-over check, and he loved leaving tips of 20 percent even when the girl was slow and sullen and splashed coffee on his newspaper. His sales, his work, his vocation, that was all bonus. The waiting, the handshakes, the lunches, The Close, jeepers, that was just icing.

If you asked Rick Bozack what he did for a living, he wouldn't come out with a song and dance about selling expensive incubators and heart and kidney machines for Doctor's Service Supply Company, Indianapolis. Not off the top of his head he wouldn't. Instead he'd flash on a motel lobby with all the salesmen in their sharp tailored

80

suits, chewing sugarless gum, while the sweet thing behind the counter rammed a roller over a plastic credit card and after-shaves mingled in the air. It was goofy when he thought about it, but walking out through those fingerprinted glass doors, throwing his briefcase onto the red bucket seat, scraping the frost off the windshield, and seeing all those other guys out there in the parking lot with him, grimacing, chipping away at their wipers, blowing on their fingers, sliding their heater controls to Defrost, he felt like a team player again, like he was part of a fighter squadron.

What was this Death of a Salesman crap? he'd say.

What were they feeding everybody about the hard life on the road?

You'd have to be zonkers not to love it.

Then Rick had a real turnaround. A college buddy said something that really clobbered him. Rick and his wife, Jane, had returned to South Bend, his home, for the Notre Dame alumni picnic, and they had collided there with people they hadn't even thought of in years. They sat all night at a green picnic table with baked beans and hot dogs and beer, laughing so much their sides hurt, having a whale of a good time together. They swapped pictures of their kids and Rick drew a diagram of an invention he might get patented, which would rinse out messy diapers for daddies right there in the toilet bowl. He told all comers that he was thirty-four years old and happily married, the father of two girls, and he woke up every morning with a sapsucker grin on his face. Then Mickey Hogan, this terrific buddy in advertising who had just started up his own firm, said you don't know the thrill of business until it's your own, until every sale you make goes directly into your pocket and not to some slob back in the home office.

This guy Hogan wasn't speaking *de profundis* or anything, but Rick was really blown away by what he said. It was one of those fuzzy notions you carry with you for years and then it's suddenly there, it's got shape and bulk and annoying little edges that give you a twinge when you sit down. That's how it was. He and Jane talked about it all the way back to their three-bedroom apartment on Rue Monet in Indianapolis. "How much of what I earn actually makes my wallet any fatter? What do I have besides an income? When am I going to get off my duff and get something going on my own?"

Jane was great about it. She said it was his decision and she loved him and she'd go along with whatever his choice was, but she had watched him waste himself at Doctor's Service Supply Company, Indianapolis. She knew he was a great salesman but he had all the earmarks of a fantastic manager too. She had been hoping he'd come up with something like this but didn't want to influence him one way or the other. "I don't want to push," were her words.

Jane's enthusiasm put a fire under Rick and he began checking things out on the sly: inventory costs, car leases and office space rentals, government withholding tax and F.I.C.A. regulations, and though it seemed dopey and juvenile, the couple decided that they'd both stop smoking, watch their caloric intake, avoid between-meal treats, and exercise regularly. Sure they were mainly concerned with hashing out this new business venture, but how far afield was it to take stock of yourself, your physical condition, to discipline yourself and set goals? That was Rick's comment and Jane thought he was "right on the money."

The two of them let a half-gallon of ice cream melt down in the stainless steel sink, got out the scale and measuring tape, bought matching jogging outfits and they took turns with Tracy and Connor at breakfast while one of them jogged around the block.

And Rick was no slouch when on the road. He jogged in strange cities and on gravel country roads and in parking lots of motels. Other salesmen would run at him in sweatbands and heavy T-shirts and Rick would say, "How's it going?"

"How's it going?" they'd reply.

Rick imagined millions of joggers saying the same things to each other. It felt as good as the days of the Latin Mass, when you knew it was just as incomprehensible in Dusseldorf, West Germany, or Ichikawa, Japan.

On one of his business trips to South Bend, he jogged on the cinder track of Notre Dame's football stadium, where who should he see but Walter Herdzina, a terrific friend of his! Rick was flabbergasted. The guy had aged—who hadn't?—but he remembered Rick like it was only yesterday, even recited some wild dorm incidents that Rick had put the blackboard eraser to. The two men ran an eight-minute mile together and leaned on their knees and wiped their faces on their sweatshirts, and after they had discussed pulse rates, refined sugar, and junk foods, his buddy Walter Herdzina said, "You ought to move back to South Bend."

Jane, bless her heart, kept bringing up South Bend too. It was smack in the middle of his territory, and a natural home base, but he had never really thought about South Bend much before the alumni picnic. When Head Office hired Rick they had naturally assumed he'd want a giant metropolis like Indianapolis to settle in so he could have some jam-packed leisure time, and he had never mentioned his strong links further north. And it wasn't unusual for Rick to spend three or four days in South Bend and not give anyone except his mom a call. But now there was a come-as-you-are feeling, some real hometown warmth there, which he hadn't noticed before.

In September he closed a deal with a gynecological clinic that would earn him six thousand dollars, what salesmen called The Cookies. But instead of driving home for a wingding celebration, he decided to make some business phone contacts, thank yous actually, to ride with his hot streak, see what fell in his lap. And he had an inkling maybe some doctors up there considered him somewhat remote.

So he stopped in the lobby of a downtown bank building to use its plush telephone booths. Then, on an impulse, he asked to see someone in the business loan department. A receptionist said a loan vice president could see him and Rick walked into his office and how's this for coincidence? The banker was Walter Herdzina! You could've knocked Rick over with a feather. "Boy, you're really going places," he said. Walter grinned. "They'll probably wise up and kick me downstairs again before I get the chair warm."

Rick spoke off the top of his head. He had been with Doctor's Service Supply Company, Indianapolis, for six years after three years with Johnson & Johnson. He had built up a pretty good trade representing Indiana and southern Michigan and had offers from industries in Minnesota and California to switch over to a district manager's job and a substantial boost in salary. What he wanted to know was, could a banker like Walter with years of experience and an eye for markets and money potential give him a solid reason why he shouldn't go into business for himself? Start his own distributorship?

The buddy in banking glanced at his watch and suggested they go out for lunch.

Rick figured that meant No. "This is pretty off-the-wall," he said. "I really haven't had time to analyze it or work up any kind of prospectus."

Walter put a hand on his shoulder. "Let's talk about it at lunch."

Mostly they talked about rugby. It had been a maiden sport at Notre Dame when they played it, but now it had taken the school by storm. Why? Because when you got right down to it, men liked seeing what they were made of, what kind of guts they had.

"Lessons like that stick," said Walter. "I get guys coming to me with all kinds of schemes, inventions, brilliant ideas. I can tell right away if they were ever athletes. If they never hurt themselves to win at something, well, I'm a little skeptical."

Walter ordered protein-rich halibut; Rick had the Dieter's Salad.

Rick told the banker traveler stories. He told him anecdotes about sales. He had sold insurance and mutual funds and, for a summer, automobiles, and he had discovered a gimmick, well not that, a *tool,* which hadn't failed him yet. It was called the Benjamin Franklin Close.

"Say you get a couple who're wavering over the purchase of a car. You take them into your office and close the door and say, 'Do you know what Benjamin Franklin would do in situations like this?' That's a toughie for them so you let them off the hook. You take out a tablet and draw a line down the center of the page, top to bottom. 'Benjamin Franklin,' you say, 'would list all the points in favor of buying this car and then he'd list whatever he could against it. Then he'd total things up.' The salesman handles all the benefits. You begin by saying, 'So okay, you've said your old car needs an overhaul. That's point one. You've said you want a station wagon for the kids; that's point two. You've told me that particular shade of brown is your favorite.' And so on. Once you've tabulated your pitches, you flip the tablet around and hand across the pen. 'Okay,' you tell them. 'Now Benjamin Franklin would write down whatever he had *against* buying that car.' And you're silent. As noiseless as you can be. You don't say boo to them. They stare at that blank side of the paper and they get flustered. They weren't expecting this at all. Maybe the wife will say, 'We can't afford it,' and the husband will hurry up and scribble that down. Maybe he'll say, 'It's really more than we need for city driving.' He'll glance at you for approval but you won't even nod your head. You've suddenly turned to stone. Now they're struggling. They see two reasons against and twelve reasons for. You decide to help them. You say, 'Was it the color you didn't like?' Of course not, you dope. You put that down as point three in favor. But the wife will say, 'Oh no, I like that shade of brown a lot.' You sit back in your chair and wait. You wait four or five minutes if you have to, until they're really uncomfortable, until you've got them feeling like bozos. Then you take the tablet from them and make a big show of making the tally. They think you're an idiot anyway; counting out loud won't surprise them. And when you've told them they have twelve points in favor, two points against, you sit back in your chair and let that sink in. You say, 'What do you think Benjamin Franklin would do in this situation?' You've got them cornered and they know it and they can't think of any way out because there's only one way and they never consider it. Pressed against the wall like that the only solution is for the man or woman to say, 'I— Just— Don't— *Feel*— Like— It— Now.' All the salesman can do is recapitulate. If they want to wait, if the vibes don't feel right, if they don't sense it's the appropriate thing to do, they've got him. I just don't feel like it now. There's no way to sell against that."

Walter grinned. He thought Rick might have something. Even in outline the distributorship had real sex appeal.

So that afternoon Rick drove south to Indianapolis with his CB radio turned down so he wouldn't have all the chatter, and he picked up a sitter for his two little roses and took Jane out for dinner that night, claiming he wanted to celebrate the six-thousand-dollar commission. But after they had toasted The Cookies, he sprang the deal on her, explained everything about the lunch and Walter's positive reaction, how it all fit together, fell into place, shot off like a rocket, zoomed. And what it all boiled down to was they could move to South Bend, buy a house, and in two months, three months, a year, maybe he'd have himself a business.

Jane was ecstatic. Jane was a dynamo. While Rick did the dog-and-pony show for his boss and got him to pick up the tab for a move to the heart of Rick's territory, Jane did the real work of selecting their home and supervising the movers. Then Rick walked Tracy and little

Connor from house to house down the new block in South Bend, introducing himself and his daughters to their new neighbors. There were five kids the same age on just one side of the street! Rick saw Tracy and Connor as teenagers at a backyard party with hanging lanterns and some of Rick's famous punch, and maybe two thousand four hundred boys trying to get a crack at his girls.

He drank iced tea with a stockbroker who crossed his legs and gazed out the window as Tracy tried to feed earthworms to his spaniel.

"Plenty of playmates," said Rick.

"This place is a population bomb."

"Yeah, but I love kids, don't you? I get home from a week on the road and there's nothing I like better than to roll on the floor a few hours with them."

"But your kids are girls!" the man said. He spit ice cubes back into his glass.

Rick shrugged. "I figure my wife will tell me when I should stop it."

What'd he think? Rick'd be copping feels, pawing them through their training bras? Maybe South Bend had its creepy side after all. Maybe a few of these daddies could bear some scrutiny.

Rick gave a full report to his wife, Jane, as they sat down with beers on the newly carpeted floor of the living room, telling her about all the fascinating people he had met in just a casual swing down the block. She said, "I don't know how you can just go knocking on doors and introducing yourself. I can't think what to converse about when I'm with strangers."

"That's one of the things that comes with being a traveler. You just assume you're welcome until someone tells you otherwise."

But how did that square with the uneasiness Rick Bozack felt with his old chum Mickey Hogan? A year ago Mickey had been an expensive copywriter, but then he had gone out on a limb to take over a smaller house that had been strictly an art and layout jobber and the gamble had paid off in spades. Mickey turned the firm into a real comer in South Bend, what they call in the trade a "hot shop."

But then Mickey had always been a brain. They had been rugby buddies at Notre Dame; they used to shoot snooker together and wear each other's tennis shoes and generally pal around like they were in a rowdy television commercial for some brand of beer. Now Mickey was almost skinny and as handsome as Sergio Franchi, and taking full advantage of it, don't let anybody kid you. They had doubled to the Notre Dame/Army game last season and Mickey brought along a knockout who kept sneaking her hand under Mickey's blue leg-warmer. Rick couldn't keep his eyes off her. Even Jane noticed it. "Boy, I bet she put lead in your pencil," she said.

So Rick was delighted, but amazed, when in February Mickey said he'd make the third for a terrific bunch of seats at the Notre Dame/ Marquette basketball game. Mickey was even sitting on the snow-shoveled steps of his condominium, like some company president on the skids, when Rick pulled up along the curb. And now Mickey was smoking a black cigarillo as Rick told him how astonished he was these days to see that everyone he met was about his age; they had all risen to positions of authority and he was finding they could do him some good. You always thought it was just your father who could throw a name around. Now Rick was doing it himself. And getting results! "I'm really enjoying my thirties," Rick said, and then smiled. "I've got twenty credit cards in my wallet and I don't get acne anymore."

Mickey looked at him, bored.

"Okay; maybe not twenty credit cards, but my complexion's all cleared up." Rick had forgotten how much of a jerk Mickey could be.

Rick kept the engine running and shoved the Captain and Tenille in his tape deck so Mickey could nestle with some good tunes, and he pressed the door chimes to a house the Herdzinas had just built: eighty-thousand smackers minimum. A small girl in pink underpants opened the door.

"Hi," said Rick in his Nice Man voice.

The girl shoved a finger up her nose.

Karen Herdzina hugged him hello. The hugging was a phenom-enon that was totally new to South Bend and Rick never felt he handled it well. He lingered a bit too long with women and with men he was on the lookout for a quick takedown and two points on the scoreboard.

"I'll put some hustle into Walt," she said. "Tell him to get it in gear."

Walter came out of the bedroom with a new shirt he was ripping the plastic off of. "Mickey in the car?"

Rick nodded. "But it really belts out the heat."

Walter unpinned the sleeves and the cardboards and shoved the trash into a paper sack that had the cellophane wrappers of record albums in it.

"Look at that," he said. "My wife. She goes out spending my hard-earned money on records. The Carpenters, John Denver. I don't know what gets into her sometimes."

"I kind of enjoy John Denver," said Rick.

Walter leaned into Rick as they walked to the thrumming Oldsmobile, fanning three tickets out like a heart-stopping poker hand. "How about these beauties, Richard?"

"Wow. What do I owe ya?"

He frowned, pushed the tickets in his wallet. *"De nada,"* said Walter. "Buy me a beer."

As Rick drove lickety-split to the game, he and Walter talked about their budding families. You could see it was driving Mickey bananas. Here he was a bachelor, giving up a night when he could've probably had some make-out artist in the sack, and all he was hearing was talk about drooling and potties and cutting new teeth. So as he climbed up onto the beltway, Rick introduced the topic of basketball and Walter straddled the hump in the back seat and scrunched forward to talk about the Marquette scoring threat, particularly a couple of spades who'd make All-American, easy. Mickey introduced the topic of Doctor's Service Supply Company, Indianapolis, and asked Walter if he knew Rick was considering his own distributorship.

The banker said, "Heck, I'm the one who put the gleam in his eye." He returned to the back seat and crossed his kid leather gloves in his lap. "I think that's a tremendous opportunity, Rick. Where've you gone with it lately?"

"He's been testing the waters," said Mickey.

"I've had it on the back burner until Jane and the kids get a better lay of the land," said Rick. "I think it might be a pretty good setup though. Almost no time on the road and very little selling. I'll see what it's like to stay around the house and carry those canvas money bags up to a teller window."

Walter said, "I read somewhere that every person who starts a new business makes at least one horrible mistake. Something really staggering. If you get through that and you don't get kayoed, I guess you got it made."

They were quiet for several minutes, as if in mourning for all those bankrupts who had been walloped in the past. The 8-track clicked from 3 to 4. Mickey tapped one of his black cigarillos on a thumbnail.

"You like those things?" Rick asked.

Mickey lit it with the car lighter. "Yep," Mickey said. "I like them a lot."

Rick turned into the Notre Dame parking lot. "Since I gave up smoking, I notice it all the time. This health kick's really made a difference. I'm down two notches on my belt, my clothes don't fit, and I want to screw all the time now." He switched off the ignition. "How's that for a side benefit?"

Mickey said, "You smile a lot, you know that?"

It was an okay game; nothing spectacular as far as Rick was concerned. In fact, if you conked him on the head he might even have said it was boring. Where was the teamwork? Where was the give and take? A couple of black guys were out there throwing up junk shots, making the white guys look like clods, propelling themselves up toward the basket like they were taking stairs three at a time. It went back and forth like that all night, and except for the spine-tingling Notre Dame fight songs, except for the silver flask of brandy they passed up and down the row, he wished he was in a motel room somewhere eating cheese slices on crackers.

At the final buzzer the three men filed out with the crowd, waving to other old buddies and asking them how tricks were. The Oldsmobile engine turned slowly with cold before it fired. Mickey removed The Captain and Tenille from the tape deck. Mister Sophisticated.

Rick took the crosstown and shoved in a tape of Tony Orlando. Walter was paging through one of the catalogues for Doctor's Service Supply Company, Indianapolis, when he noticed a pizza parlor was still open, how did that sound? Rick admitted it didn't blow the top of his head off but he guessed he could give it a whirl. Mickey just sat there like wax.

Rick swerved in next to a souped-up Ford with big rear wheels that looked like boulders. "Secret Storm" was printed in maroon on the fender. As they walked to the entrance, Rick saw the three of them in the reflecting front windows, in blue shirts and rep ties and two-hundred-dollar topcoats, frowns in their eyes and gray threads in their hair and gruesome mortgages on their houses.

Walter stood with Rick at the counter as he ordered a combination pizza. An overhead blower gave them pompadours. "That was fun," said Rick.

"My wife encourages me to go out with the boys. She thinks it'll keep me from chasing tail."

Rick wished he had been somewhere else when Walter said that. It said everything about the guy.

Mickey had walked to the cigarette machine and pressed every button, then, deep in his private Weltschmerz, he wandered past a sign in the restaurant that said "This Section Closed." Rick backed away from the counter with three beers, sloshing some on his coat, and made his way to the forbidden tables where Mickey was sitting.

Mickey frowned. "How long are we going to dawdle here?"

"You got something you wanted to do?"

"There's *always* something to do, Rick."

A girl in a chef's hat seated an elderly couple in the adjoining area. She had pizza menus that she crushed to her breast as she sidestepped around benches toward the drinking buddies, bumping the sign that said "This Section Closed," schoolmarm disapproval in her eyes. Mickey rocked back in his chair. "Can I just sit here for a while? Would it ruin your day if I just sat here?"

The girl stopped and threw everything she had into the question and then shrugged and walked back to the cash register.

Rick almost smacked his forehead, he was that impressed. Mickey could get away with stuff that would land Rick in jail or in small claims court.

Soon he and Walter tore into a combination pizza, achieving at once a glossy burn on the roofs of their mouths. Mickey must not have wanted any. He seemed to have lost the power of speech. After a while Walter asked the two if they had read a magazine article about a recent psychological study of stress.

Rick asked, "How do you find time to read?"

Walter said, "I can't. My wife gets piles of magazines in the mail, though, and gives me digests of them at dinner."

Mickey looked elsewhere as Walter explained that the theory of this particular study was that whenever a person shifted the furniture of his life in any significant way at all, he or she was increasing the chances of serious illness. Change for the better? Change for the worse? Doesn't matter. If your spouse dies you get a hundred points against you. You get fired, that's fifty. You accomplish something outstanding, really excellent, still you get in the neighborhood of thirty points tacked onto your score. The list went on and on. Mortgages counted, salary bonuses, shifts in eating habits. Walter said, "You collect more than three hundred of these puppies in a year and it's time to consult a shrink."

Neither Walter nor Rick could finish his pizza, so Rick asked the kitchen help for a sack to carry the remains in. Then the three men walked out into the night gripping their collars at their necks, their ears crimped by the cold. It was close to zero. They could hear it in the snow.

There were three boys in the car that was christened "Secret Storm," each dangling cheeze pizza over his mouth.

Rick opened the car door on his side and bumped the trim on the souped-up Ford. He smiled and shrugged his shoulders at the kid on the passenger's side.

The kid called him a son of a bitch.

Mickey immediately walked around the car. "What'd he call you?"

"Nothing, Mickey. He was kidding."

But Mickey was already thumping the kid's car door with his knee. "I want to hear what you called him."

The door bolted open against Mickey's camel's hair coat, soiling it, and a kid bent out unsnapping a Catholic high school letterman's jacket. Before he had the last snap undone, Mickey punched the kid in the neck. The kid grabbed his throat and coughed. Mickey held his fists like cocktail glasses.

Walter stood in the cold with his gloved hands over his ears as Rick tried to pull Mickey away from the fracas. The kid hooked a fist into Rick's ear and knocked him against the car. Mickey tackled the kid and smacked him against the pavement. Dry snow fluffed up and blew. Rick covered his sore ear and Mickey tried to pin the kid's arms with his knees but the other boys were out of the Ford by then and pleading with the kid named Vic to let the guy go. It was at once obvious to Rick that the boys weren't aware they were dealing with three virile males in the prime of their lives, who had once played rugby at Notre Dame in the days when it was just a maiden sport.

Rick and Walter managed to untangle their buddy and haul him inside the car. Rick started the engine and spun his wheels in snow as he gunned the Oldsmobile out of the place. One of the kids kicked his bumper. The others were breathing on their hands.

"I don't believe it," said Rick.

Mickey was huffing; no jogger, he. "You don't believe what?" Mickey said.

"You're thirty-five years old, Mick! You don't go banging high school kids around."

Walter wiped the back window with his glove. "Oh no," he groaned.

Mickey turned around. "Are they following us?"

"Maybe their home's in the same direction," said Rick.

Mickey jerked open the door. Cold air flapped through the catalogues of Doctor's Service Supply Company, Indianapolis. "Let me out," Mickey said.

"Are you kidding?" Rick gave him a look that spoke of his resolute position on the question while communicating his willingness to compromise on issues of lesser gravity.

And yet Mickey repeated, "Let me out."

"What are you going to do?"

"Shut up and let me out of this car."

Walter said, "I think those are *Catholic* kids, Michael."

They were on a potholed residential street of ivied brick homes and one-car garages. There were white globes on eight-foot green streetlamps. Rick made a right-hand turn and so did the other car.

Mickey pushed the door wide open and scraped off the top of a snow pile. He leaned out toward the curb like a sick drunk about to lose it until Rick skidded slantwise on the ice pack and stopped. Then Mickey trotted out and slipped on the ice and sprawled against the right front door of the Ford.

The boy named Vic cracked his noggin on the doorframe trying to get out and he sat back down pretty hard, with tears in his eyes and both hands rubbing his hair.

"All right, you bastard," the driver said, and lurched out, tearing off *his* letterman's jacket. (Rick had worked like hell and never got one. And there weren't any razzle-dazzle black kids around then either.) The third kid got out and put his hand in his jeans pocket. He stripped a stick of gum and folded it in his mouth. Rick walked over to him and the kid's eyes slid. "Bob's going to make mincemeat out of your friend, man."

Mickey and the kid named Bob stepped over a yard hedge and Mickey was now hanging his coat on a clothesline pole. Walter was on the sidewalk stamping snow off his wing tips.

"Can you believe this weather?" Rick asked the kid. "My nose is like an ice cube."

The kid smiled. "Colder than a witch's tit, ain't it?"

The kid was in Rick's pocket. Rick still had the goods, all right.

Mickey and the boy named Bob were closing in the night-blue back yard like boxers about to touch gloves, when Mickey swung his fist into the kid's stomach and the kid folded up like a cardtable chair. "Ow! Oh man, where'd you hit me? Geez, that hurts."

A light went on in an upstairs bathroom.

Vic got out of the car, still holding his head, and the other kid tripped through the snow to help Bob limp to the Ford. "Get me to a hospital quick!"

"Oh, you're okay, Bob," said Vic.

"You don't know, man! I think he might've burst my appendix or something! I think he was wearing a ring!"

Mickey carefully put on his coat and sucked the knuckles of his hand when he sat down inside the car. Rick drove to Mickey's condominium first. Mickey was touching a bump on his forehead, smirking in Rick's direction.

"What made you want to do that, Mick?"

"Are you going to let some punk call you a son of a bitch?"

Rick slapped the steering wheel. "Of course! I do it all the *time*. Is that supposed to destroy you or something?"

Mickey just looked at the floormats or out the window. He jumped out when Rick parked in front of his place, and he didn't say goodbye.

Walter seated himself in the front bucket seat. "Whew! What an evening, huh?"

"I feel like I've run fourteen miles."

Walter crossed his legs and jiggled his shoe until Rick drove onto Walter's driveway whereupon he shook Rick's hand and suggested they do this again sometime and also wished him good luck in getting his business out of the starting gate.

The light was on in the upstairs bedroom of the Bozacks' blue Colonial home. Jane had switched the lights off downstairs. Rick let himself in with the milk box key and hung up his coat. He opened and shut the refrigerator door and then found himself patting his pockets for cigarettes. He went to the dining room breakfront and found an old carton of Salems.

He got a yellow ruled tablet and a pen from the desk and sat down in the living room with a lit cigarette. He printed VENTURE at the top. He drew a line down the center of the paper and numbered the right-hand side from one to twelve. After a few minutes there, Jane came down the stairs in her robe.

"Rick?"

"What?"

"I wanted to know if it was you."

"Who else would it be?"

"Why don't you come up? I'm only reading magazines."

"I think I'd like to just sit here for a while."

"In the *dark?*"

He didn't speak.

"Are you smoking?"

"Yep. I was feeling especially naughty."

She was silent. She stood with both feet on the same step. "You're being awfully mysterious."

"I just want to sit here for a while. Can I do that? Can I just sit here for a while?"

Jane climbed the stairs to their bedroom.

Rick stared at the numbered page. Why quit the team? Why risk the stress? Why give up all those cookies.

If pressed against the wall he'd say, "I just don't feel like it now."

Blessing

Elizabeth Stuckey-French

T HE DAY after New Year's, late in the afternoon, Riley gives into himself and decides to go looking for arrowheads. He invites his son Matt, who is stretched out on the living room couch, to come with him. Riley makes the outing sound as enticing as possible, mentioning exercise, fresh air, history, and artifacts.

"Whatever," Matt mumbles from under his afghan. He pokes his head out and glares at Riley. *The Sun Also Rises* slides off the leather couch and plops on the carpet. Matt is home for Christmas break. He goes out every night with his high school sweetheart Heather, and then naps all day on the couch.

Riley taps a rolled map against his thigh, waiting, till Matt kicks the afghan aside, displaying soiled grey sweatpants and bare chest. Matt is a head taller than his father, and has his mother's dark hair and olive complexion. Riley is a redhead with fair skin. He's wearing flannel-lined jeans and a Pendleton shirt. He feels like he and Matt have stepped out of different movie sets.

Matt sits up and stretches. "Let's take Kip," he says, yawning.

When Matt has dressed and slung a windbreaker over his shoulder, Riley slips on his down jacket and they head into the kitchen. The kitchen, with its copper-colored appliances and brick-red floor, always

95

looks and feels like the warmest room in the house. Now it smells like hot chocolate.

Just back from aerobics, Riley's wife Marlene and Heather are settled at the table, clipping articles from magazines and filing them in manilla folders. Heather's helping Marlene with a project for her master's thesis—a national survey of farm wives to discover how they've coped with the farm crisis. Riley can't help but notice how Heather fits right into their family, better than their own daughter ever has.

"We're going on an expedition," Riley announces.

Marlene, in her pink velour sweat suit, flips off her reading glasses and lets them fall on the chain around her neck. "To that Indian village, I bet."

According to the historical map Marlene gave Riley for Christmas, the site of what once was the largest Indian settlement in Indiana is just ten miles from their farm.

"Boys only?" Heather asks Matt, her scissors dangling open. Heather's green and white striped leotard molds her body. Her dark hair twirls in shiny corkscrews. Matt whispers in Heather's ear, then kisses her twice on the lips.

"Need to take provisions?" Marlene asks Riley over the rim of her mug. Steam curls around her face.

"We'll be back in a couple hours for dinner." Riley bends down and pecks her cheek.

Marlene gathers up her stack of folders and taps them on the table to straighten them. "Don't look too hard, or you won't find one."

Riley's been looking for arrowheads since he was a boy walking beans on his grandfather's farm in Iowa. When he and his father hunted quail along Wildcat Creek, Riley scanned the banks for arrowheads. With Marlene, he searched the Arizona desert on a cross-country trip in '67. At age forty-nine, while disking his fields, Riley still keeps an eye out. So far, he hasn't found one.

Many times Riley imagines the moment—suddenly spotting a chiseled tip poking up through the earth, his hand reaching out. Finding an arrowhead has come to mean the same as having a vision—being singled out for something important. But he can't explain this to anyone.

"If we don't look, we damn sure won't find one," he says.

Marlene slips her glasses back on. "Well, that's true, too." Then, as Riley's closing the door behind them, she calls, "How's The Beef House sound for dinner?"

Matt drives his Accord, a high school graduation present. Riley sits beside him, feeling bulky and clumsy. Kip presses his muzzle against the back window. They bounce down gravel roads between velvet black fields, then turn north on Division Highway, which after five miles becomes River Road. The sky curving over them is cloudless, Dutch blue.

"Great weather," Riley says. "First day the sun's been out in a month. Not one inch of snow yet this year. But then last year we didn't get a good one till February. Maybe the atmosphere's heating up. I read that somewhere. Greenhouse effect."

"It snowed in Bloomington," Matt says. He's frowning at the tape deck, punching fast forward, letting out blurts of music, then fast forwarding again.

A man on a motorcycle putters up beside them. Matt reaches for the tape box and their car drifts toward the cyclist. Matt looks up and pulls the wheel back. The man gives them the finger and accelerates.

"Guy belongs in a nuthouse," Riley says, gripping the door handle.

"Does Mom ever come up for air?"

"Once in a while. She's busier now than she's ever been. Here's the turn."

Matt downshifts and swings left onto a rutted gravel road. "We used to come out here," he shouts over the music and the rocks flipping against the undercarriage. "Back in high school."

Riley turns down the music. "What?"

"Never mind." On both sides of the road, yellow prairie grass lies flat, matted down by frost. As they creak over the wooden planks of Granville Bridge, Riley looks down through rusty iron bars at the Wabash. Muddy water swirls under them, sweeping along chunks of ice like giant blobs of wax.

Riley has a print of Bingham's "Fur Traders Descending the Missouri" in his den. In his mind, they're descending the Wabash. He belts out, "Through the sycamores the candlelight is gleaming, on the banks of the Wabash, far away, . . ." He waits for Matt to join in. Matt was in the Glee Club in high school. But now he keeps silent, staring straight ahead, and Riley trails off, self-conscious.

They clank off the bridge, pass the chalky white sycamores lining the bank, and start uphill between two fields of dry corn husks.

"I heard that's a top notch bird spot." Riley points up ahead to a grove of trees, purple against the sky. "Let's bring Kip out here next fall. He misses you." Riley reaches back and scratches Kip's ear. Kip's tail thumps at the sound of his name.

"Wish I had more weekends free. I do miss hunting. Did you go this year?"

"Not once." Riley tries to sound casual, but fails. He reasserts himself. "Why don't we pull off here? Right here's where the Indian village was. The Wea Plain. We can walk along the edge of these fields a ways."

"You got it, Patches." Last summer Matt found pictures of Riley, pictures Riley kept in the bottom of the file cabinet and hadn't even shown Marlene. Bathing suits, beer, women. And Riley with bushy black sideburns—patches. Riley grabs the back of Matt's neck and squeezes.

"Cut it out." Matt elbows Riley.

For a moment Riley feels twenty years lighter. "Park!"

"Yes, sir!" Matt wheels over on the left side of the road. They climb out, hunching their shoulders in the cold air. Riley opens the back door for Kip, who leaps out and sniffs furiously around the front tire.

Matt zips up the light windbreaker over a football letter sweater he borrowed from Riley. The knees of his thin army pants ripple in the wind. "Which way?"

"Well, let's see." Riley swivels on the heel of his workboot. "The Indian camp went both ways along the river here." He pauses for effect. "But let's go right. With the wind, since you didn't dress warm."

Matt whirls and stalks off across the field, Kip trotting beside him.

"This is like hitchhiking in a snowstorm," Riley says as he catches up to them. "Your destination changes with the way the cars are going."

Matt knits his thick eyebrows together and scrunches his mouth to one side. Weird, his face says.

"Let's go to the top of this field and look along the edge," Riley says. "The Indians farmed 400 acres of squash and corn here. We might find all sorts of things. Who knows?"

"Who knows?"

Turning right, they walk uphill, stepping over the furrows. Kip weaves between them, tail waving like a metronome. Wind numbs the inch of flesh between Riley's Pioneer Seed cap and his scarf. He wriggles snugly in his thermal underwear. He notices that Matt's naked ears, under his spiked black hair, glow pink.

At the top of the field they curve left, walking parallel to the river, hidden by woods three hundred yards below them. A string of maple trees on their right separates this field from the next field up. They stop to look between the trees at a white two-story farmhouse which is nearly identical to theirs. "Whose land is this?" Matt asks.

"Belongs to the head of IBM. He bought up the riverfront land this side of Granville bridge clear up to Lilly's as an investment. Along here should be a good place for arrowheads." Riley squats down, picking at a rock with his gloved fingers.

They creep along, bent over, scanning the ground. The corn here, like that on Riley's land, has been plowed under. But here the soil is sandy—brown flakes frosted with ice crystals. Riley tugs at a rock frozen in the ground. He stamps his foot. It's like stamping on iron. He kicks the rock, a flint he'd hoped at first was an arrowhead. His big toe stings. He should have waited till spring.

Riley had mentioned the Indian village to Marlene's brother, Simms, while they were dawdling over coffee one morning at the Grand Prairie Cafe. Simms gave advice, as usual. "Spring's the best time to look. Thaw'll bring arrowheads to the surface."

But Riley couldn't wait till spring. He sold the hogs two years ago. They canceled their annual trip to Orlando because of Marlene's classes, and all that's on his schedule is church league basketball.

"These things are really in there," Matt says, chipping away at the dirt with a stick.

Riley decides he and Matt should talk about something important. Marlene'll want a report tonight. Matt's their quiet child, the one who keeps his distance. Not like their daughter, Lynn, a potter in Nag's Head, who tells them more than they want to know.

"How's school?" Riley's eyes mechanically sweep the ground.

"Better than being slapped in the face with a wet fish, I guess."

"Where you gonna apply to law school?"

"Don't know."

"Hmmm." Getting Matt to talk seriously about himself is like prying the rocks out of the ground.

"What kind of Indians lived here, anyway?" Matt asks.

"Middle Mississippian. Then Miami and Potawatami. This is the only place in the country where Plains, Mississippian and Algonquin Indians came together," Riley says, realizing he took the bait.

They examine pink rocks, grey ones, rusty brown ones. Riley has a sinking feeling he won't find an arrowhead today—that he might never find one.

Last year Simms tried to give Riley a shoebox full of projectile points, knives, and scrapers he'd found on his Warren County farm. "From the prehistoric Middle Mississippian culture," Simms had said, worrying an arrowhead in his worm-colored fingers.

"I can tell that. Thanks, but keep 'em," Riley said. Simms couldn't understand the importance of finding them yourself.

"How come you quit going to church?" Matt says.

"Haven't."

"You didn't go today."

"Don't like the new minister. I'm taking a leave of absence."

"He's a redneck." Matt crouches on his haunches, his breath puffing out like cigarette smoke. "I can't say that to Mom. She'd have a shit fit."

"OK, Bud, enough. Watch your mouth." Riley sounds firmer than he feels. He remembers the Sunday last month he'd sat in the congregation because he missed choir rehearsal. Three pews ahead sat Dawn, the minister's wife. Riley marveled at the fact that her neck could have been any neck. It evoked no memory of the evening he and Dawn spent in the church lounge with the door locked. He knew now that it had been an attempt to capture something that was never there, and he assumed that Dawn knew the same.

As they stood to sing the benediction, Riley watched Marlene, singing with her shoulders thrown back, breasts straining against the scarlet choir robe. Their eyes met, and Marlene's lips bloomed in a smile. Riley winked back.

During the postlude when he turned to leave, Riley felt Dawn staring at him. She blocked one end of his pew, so he edged out the other end. He hasn't been back to church since then.

Matt and Riley approach the end of the field, now walking briskly. They brush through a grove of saplings, bare branches whipping at them, and into a clearing. Logs form a circle in the dry leaves, as if someone had once planned to make a bonfire and forgot. Riley plops down on a log. His neck aches from looking at the ground.

"Wanna keep going? I'm plenty warm," Matt says, hopping on one foot and then the other, bare ankles flashing. His cheeks are flushed.

"Sure. Hey, where's Kip?" Riley jumps up. He fights down a wave of panic, the same way he did when the kids got lost at the state fair. "Kip! Here Kipper!" He cups his hands around his mouth and yells in every direction.

Matt does the same. "Kip! Here boy!"

Kip's barking, faint but ecstatic, comes from the river.

"He's swimming," Matt says, and smiles at Riley.

"We'd better go get him."

They set off out of the grove and start down a soybean field toward the river.

"Does he swim much?" Matt asks.

"No. Never thought of bringing him here. Not that I have the time."

"He'd love it."

"Feel free to bring him yourself."

"Sorry. Just a suggestion."

Kip belongs to both of them. The summer after Matt's junior year in high school, Riley, Marlene and Matt went to visit Lynn and Sara in their beach cottage. Riley and Matt spent hours throwing a stick for Sara's Chesapeake Bay Retriever. They loved his red kinky coat and little pig eyes, and they loved the fact that his ancestors swam to the Eastern Shore of Virginia after a shipwreck, origins unknown.

Riley and Matt decided they should have a Chesapeake. That

winter they studied breeder's information, and in March they drove to the Eastern Shore for their puppy. They named him Kiptopeke, after the town he was born in.

As they near the bottom of the field, the muddy river smell rises up to meet them. The earth becomes wetter and softer, and the wind dies down.

"Hey," Matt says. He scrapes his deck shoe along a row of dried bean plants.

"Yes?"

"Are you and Mom down about Lynn and Sara?"

"No. We don't think about it."

"Just checking."

Riley realizes he's grinding his teeth, something the dentist warned him against. He relaxes his jaw. "Don't say that to your mom. Kip!" Riley calls, and Kip woofs in reply.

They enter the woods where the remnants of the Wabash and Erie canal, now a line of unconnected ditches, lie between them and the river. Riley picks his way through the underbrush, skirting a frozen ditch.

Matt stops at the ditch, pushing down with one foot at the edge, testing. The ice cracks below the surface with a dull twang. "You could skate on these babies," he yells.

Riley turns around to see Matt inching his way onto the ice. "That's not gonna hold you."

Matt steps back to the bank and picks up a rock. He sends it skittering over the ice, making a hollow ringing sound. "Cool."

Riley continues around the ditch, pressing on towards the river, pushing aside the brittle cane towering above his head, crunching cattails beneath his feet.

"Dad!" Matt is sidling across the trunk of a tree hanging across the ditch, as if he's walking a tightrope. He waves at Riley, then gyrates to keep his balance. Riley imagines Matt falling, the way he fell off the gate when he was three and had to have five stitches in his forehead. Riley turns away.

When he reaches the river bank, Riley steps between the sycamore trees. Kip is swimming in circles, fighting the current, yipping and splashing. His breath steams in a cloud over his head.

Riley feels his shoulders loosen. Kip is a born swimmer. Swimming is one thing he didn't have to be taught. Riley remembers the day he and Matt went to visit Kip at the training camp in Virginia. They watched Kip retrieve dummies from an unmowed field, then walked him back to the kennel with the trainer. The dogs in the kennel stopped barking instantly when the trainer said "Quiet."

"Wow! How'd you teach 'em that?" Matt said.

"The pens are electric," the trainer said. "They learn."

Riley glanced at his son, wishing Matt hadn't asked. Matt's eyes darted to Riley's face, then away. He jerked around and began stroking the nose of a black Lab through a metal gate. "Good boy, good boy," he said.

Matt pops up beside Riley on the river bank. "Kip's having the time of his life," he says, breathing hard.

"I'll try to take him swimming once in a while."

They sit down on the hard ground together. Beginning at their toes, paper-thin sheets of ice slope down towards the river where the water has receded. Riley breaks off a piece, imprinted with the outline of a leaf. He flicks his wrist and the ice shatters on the rocks with a tinkling sound. From the lower branches of the sycamore trees, icicles hang in uniform rows like the candles Marlene makes at Christmas. On the opposite bank is the town of Riverview. A grain elevator, then railroad tracks, then a church and two rows of houses huddle together, as if for protection against the river and the prairie. In a mud lot beside the grain elevator sits a row of identical white trailers, each with a different color trim—red, blue, yellow. The smell of burning trash drifts over the water.

"Can you keep a secret?" Matt says.

Riley knows this is something else he doesn't want to hear. "I'll try."

Matt's chewing the inside of his cheek, a habit he picked up from Marlene. "Heather and I are engaged."

"You're too young," Riley says, then wishes he'd thought first.

"We're not getting married till next summer."

"I mean can't you wait till you finish school? Till you know what you want?" The picture of Matt and Heather living together, playing house, is almost as upsetting as that of Lynn and Sara in their beach cottage.

"Heather's the one thing I'm sure of," Matt says, cracking an ice sheet with his heel. "You and Mom got married when you were in college."

"I'd been in the Navy four years," Riley says, knowing it hadn't made any difference. "When will you tell your mother?"

"Tonight. I want your blessing, Dad." The words sound stilted coming from Matt.

A flash of white on the opposite bank catches Riley's eye. A hawk floats up from the brush, then begins slowly pumping its wings. A string of red entrails swings from its beak.

"Matt." Riley points at the hawk, now disappearing over some trees, blackened and backlit by the setting sun.

"You and Mom are happy."

"Uh huh."

"We'll live in married student housing. We'll both work and go to school part time. When we graduate, we want to go out West. Like you two did."

The cold is seeping up through Riley's pants. He stands and gives Matt a hand up. "Let's go."

Without calling for Kip, they walk back through the trees at an angle, towards the car. Riley hears Kip paddle to the shore, shake himself, and thrash through the cane after them. They come upon an abandoned trailer, its moss green paint still showing between rust spots.

"Did someone actually live in this?" Matt asks.

"Maybe used it for a fishing camp."

"Strange." Matt slumps on ahead, his hands in his pockets, suddenly looking ten years older.

Riley examines the empty shell of the trailer—the rotting wooden floor, rusty smokestack, ladder propped against the side—as if searching for an explanation.

"Look here." Matt bends down beside a tree where Kip is sniffing at something.

Riley crosses over to them. Small silvery fish, like half dollars with black filmy eyes, are papered against the bottom and sides of a dried puddle. "They must've got caught when the river went down," Riley says. He pokes at one, the belly spongy and the tail stiff, frozen to the ground. "They're either little crappies or sunfish. I'll look 'em up when we get home."

Matt straightens up and backs away. "I really don't expect you to have all the answers."

They tramp on through the woods. Riley wraps his arm around Matt's shoulders. "It's just that we worry about you, okay?"

"I know," Matt says. He sighs. "I worry about you, too."

They walk out into the field. A thin mist, like steam, swirls over the ground. In the middle of the field is a frozen puddle as big as a pond. Matt lopes toward it. He stomps along the edge, making little puddles. Kip trails him, slurping up the water.

Riley steps onto the ice, gingerly at first. His stomach lurches when his right boot slips through with a crunch. Farther out, the ice is bubbled but solid. Riley begins to slide, first slowly, then he runs to build up speed. He sails down the length of the puddle. "Come on out, Matt." Wind whips the words from his mouth.

He turns to see Matt standing in the center of the puddle, watching him. Matt begins to tap dance, knocking his heels and toes on the ice, spinning in circles.

Riley runs as fast as he can towards Matt, then lunges and slides, leaning into it. "Whooo!"

Matt is bent double laughing. He holds out his arms to protect himself. Riley, still sliding, crouches down and bear-hugs Matt's knees. Matt flops on top of Riley and they roll over and over on the ice, pretending to wrestle. Then they untangle themselves and collapse flat on their backs, still heaving with laughter. Kip crouches, rump hiked up, barking.

"Well, it's getting dark," Riley finally says. "We'd better head back."

But they lie side by side, staring up at the now pale sky, rippling with grey-peaked clouds, like waves.

"I've got an arrowhead if you want one," Matt says. "Found it detasseling last year."

"Thanks, son."

The wind groans in the trees, and Riley feels sweat freezing on his neck. He sits up, leaning back on his hands. Below the clouds, Venus glows like a silver bead in the dark blue sky, and below that, the gold light warms to apricot. Smoke curls up from black roofs in Riverview. Riley thinks of his split oak, stacked neatly beside the stove at home. Suddenly bells twang out, tinny and hollow, from a church across the river.

"What's that hymn?" Matt says, lifting his head. He starts humming.

Riley listens. The tune is familiar, one that he has heard all of his life. He tries to think of the words, but he can't remember them. Instead he begins to hum softly, along with Matt.

The First Winter of My Married Life

William H. Gass

THE FIRST winter of our married life, we lived in a slum near the edge of the Wabash. The university had thrown up half-a-dozen prefabricated duplexes during the war and rented them out to the faculty whom it also impoverished in other ways. The war was over. I had persuaded Martha to marry me. I carried certain glorious credentials, and we were both ready to make a start in life, as the saying was then. It proved a bitter winter in every respect. We lived side by side with a fellow from biology: his sink butted our sink; his john rubbed the rear of ours; the shower stalls were linked; and we shared laundry and storage sheds like a roller-towel in a public lavatory. Our garbage went in a common can and we parked our cars nose to tail in the street like sniffing dogs. Often the mailman got our letters mixed.

In front, the property was divided in fair-minded halves the way Solomon, in his wisdom, would surely have apportioned it (around their gum tree they planted crocus bulbs, while around our Chinese elm we put in daffs); but the backyard was enclosed by a weak wire fence which any gumptious turf would have shoved aside in a single season. There our lawn lay in pale passivity while weeds pushed through its flimsy sod like the spikes of a florist's frog. We were conscientious renters, though, and by unspoken agreement, took carefully measured turns to mow the dandelions and plantain down.

The walls were thin, and soon we were sharing our quarrels too. The sounds of love-making passed between us like cups of borrowed sugar, and cooking odors were everywhere like the same paint. When the cold water tap on our tub was first turned, a shudder went through the pipe to which it was attached, it seemed to me, all the way to the reservoir. A single furnace fired us, but somehow all our ducts were tangled, so that the moans and groans of the house would wander like lost souls, carried through them on the warm rising air, to emerge with a bright irrelevant clarity (". . . on the sofa . . ." "Carrie called . . ." ". . . later . . .-n't the time . . .") in any odd place at all and abruptly as a belch—occasionally even returning to the room where they'd been made—echoes as battered as our cooking pans.

When we met on the walk outside, often hugging groceries or lugging books—just because we heard our toilets flush—we scarcely spoke, our heads hidden behind redly stenciled paper sacks; and in the laundry room, encounters were so brief and polite the gas man knew us better. Martha's ardor oddly came and went, and although I knew it was connected with the goings-on next door, it did not simply wax and wane with them; the correlation was more complicated, duplicitous, remote.

We were soon ashamed of our own sounds, as if every sign of life we made were a form of breaking wind. We were ashamed because we believed we heard the pop and creak of their floors, their stairs and settling springs, when normally we never noticed our own; because the scream of their kettle called us to our quiet kitchen; because we struggled to restore some sense to the voices which burbled and rumbled behind our common walls as one strains a pulpy juice for jelly; and we had to assume that they were curious too, had exchanged lewd grins, held fingers aside their noses like Santa Claus in that stupid poem, and had at least once listened through a wine glass to passages of passion of one kind or other. They would have been mostly about money, then, for at that time we hadn't any, nor could we hear any harmony in the loose rattle of our change; so we fought like children about whether we should spend or save.

Martha kept faith in a challenging future. I lapsed like an unpaid policy. Hence Martha conserved while I consumed. She sold. I bought. She bawled me out. She wanted me to quit smoking. It was a selfish habit, she said. She claimed we couldn't afford to buy books or pay dues in my damn clubs or fees for regular checkups. Nothing's going to go wrong with a nice soft body like yours, she said, palping me like a roasting turkey. The university's library was large. There were lots of free lectures, and all the good movies would come round again like the famous comets. But who wants to watch a film as ancient as the family album? who cares about last year's lovers, or all those stabbings stale as buns, or auto chases on worn-out tires, I said, exasperation showing in my prose.

But we cut back. We inspected the dates on our pennies. I felt like a shabby freeloader, attending receptions just to snuffle up the cake and cookies, pocket mints. We kept magazines until they were old enough to be reread; converted boxes, cans, and jars, by means of découpage, a little sanding and shellac, into jaundiced baskets, pencil crocks, and letter bins—Christmas presents for the folks which only cost us our pride. I licked her slender vaginal lips like a Roman emperor. The simple pleasures are the best, she said. I cadged returnables from our neighbor's trash; she returned the empties, saved trading stamps, suggested an extensive use of departmental stationery, the department phone for distant friends. Off and on I'd hunger for a steak, a melon, or a mound of shrimp. I think the wine we drank was trampled in Vermont.

Indiana's cold came down the river like a draft, and the deep gray sky grew closer every day. Chimney smoke seemed simply an extension of it, as did one's steaming breath. I had suffered many a Midwest winter, but I had never been married to the snow. During an embrace, I would discover my arm clamped about my wife's waist like a frozen limb.

At first the snow helped. It kept us in. We played parcheesi to calm our nerves. Martha would cook chicken livers again, and then, because they were so cheap—dear god—immediately again. She recommended peanut butter and claimed beans were a good buy. They blow balloons up your ass, I'd shout, with an embarrassed unoriginality, and then we would both look warily up and down, ducking my outcry as if I'd just hurled a tennis ball against the wall. In this toilet-tissue house, I'd hiss poisonously in her ear, we can't afford to fart. Then even when there was boot-deep snow, a cold scarf of wind, I'd leave the place to pout, closing the front door cautiously, violence in my silent face.

They'd designed our building like a pair of paper mittens, but the left mitten had been limp when we moved in, otherwise we might have been warned; and when its new tenants arrived, we found nothing amiss in the movers' tread or the gruff reality of their voices. The clear scrape of cardboard cartons did not trouble us, or the thump of heavy chests. Besides, it was warm, and windows were open. We simply had new neighbors. There was a hand now stuffed in the other glove. The noise was natural. Things would settle down. We hoped they would prove to be sympathetic types, maybe even friends. Then a head-board bumped rhythmically against what we'd thought was our most private wall. Their vacuum cleaner approached and receded like a train. Waters were released which gushed and roared and even whistled. Didn't I hear a male voice singing "Lazy Mary" one morning? Whose life could ever be the same?

After that we tiptoed, grew footpads, became stealthy. When we heard their closest hangers jangle like cattle on a hill far away, we shut our doors so silently the latches snicked like a rifle. I had heard his heavy smoker's hack (hollow, deep, and wet as a well), so we took multivitamins to ward off coughs, then syrups to stifle them when colds caught us anyway, and increasingly felt like thieves and assassins.

Our ears were soon as sensitive as a skinless arm, and we spoke in whispers, registered the furtive drip of remote taps. It was like living in front of a mike as you might pose and smirk in front of a mirror. We heard ourselves as others might hear us; we read every sound the way we read the daily paper; and we came to feel as though we were being chased, caught, charged, and humiliatingly arraigned for crimes against the public silence—for making obscene sounds at the symphony or crying out loud at the circus.

In the flush of our shame, we wanted no one to know us, so we held hats in front of our voices, coats over our sinks and drains. We treated even the crudest iron cooking pot as if it were Limoges, slowing our motions as movies had shown us we should to defuse explosives. I ceased singing in the shower. We kissed only in distant corners, and as quietly as fish. We gave up our high-spirited games. Martha no longer cried out when she came, and I grew uncertain of her love. Small incidents were absurdly enlarged the way the whine of a mosquito is magnified by an enclosing darkness: a fallen spoon sounded like a broken jar, a shattered glass was a spilled tray, a dropped book a bomb. I exaggerate now, but it's true that as our neighbors sensed our presence the way we had theirs, they sent their sounds to Coventry too, and the house was shortly filled—palpably stuffed—with silence like a stomach's ache.

I began to suffer from insomnia. The dark boneless hollow of our bedroom seemed the menacing shape of my future, and I stared into it as if the energy of my eyes would act as a light. Maybe, less than a forearm away, another husband was doing the same—one whole half of his hopes discovered to be empty as a soldier's sleeve. It was not the kind of commencement I had counted on. I thought of my career (it was the commonest cliché) as one great climb—stretches of superhuman effort spelled by brief stops for rest and acclimation. People and towns would assume their true size, dwindling like the past behind me, becoming merely part of the grand patterns of history. I knew I would have to strain every nerve (as it was uncomfortably put) to realize my ambitions. A simple inspection of the past was child's play, but the composition of history was not a young man's work; it was not an arena for the display of an ill-informed or immature mind; no inept cape, however flamboyant, could turn aside the charges of time; it was not everybody's satisfying hobby or soothing Sunday scribble; for how many great ones were there in a century? when poets were as plentiful as pilchards and paintings bloomed like fields of fall weeds. I would have to climb beyond bias, become Olympian, part the clouds; and already I had resolved to work with material so racial and rednecked and cruel and costly (the extirpation of the Jews exceeded any subject), what tools or gloves or masks or prophylactic washing-up would protect me from contamination? It was not like the commitment of the poet, whose projects were likely to last as long as his latest erection—whether for elegy, ode, or little lyric—or till the clit was rubbed like an angry correction.

I suddenly realized, considering this, that perhaps I spent so readily because I felt more secure in my future, while Martha conserved because she felt she hadn't any.

Home life (ho hum life, my colleague, Culp, insisted) . . . the home

. . . The orphanage in my home town was called The Home. The home was supposed to be a help: a place of rest and solace you returned to at night and went forth from refreshed like a watered plant. Despite the fact that my childhood home had been nothing like that, and although I had the satisfying cynicism of a young man who has read about more evil than he's seen, and even though I already had the deepest misgivings about every form of human relation; nevertheless, I hadn't married to be miserable, to be picked apart by fury and malice, crushed by common chores; I fully expected to inhabit such a place of peace and pleasure: a castle, a home, an Eden.

. . . within which the body of one's wife warmed and restored, as it had the elders of Israel from the beginning. The magic of her scented flesh made you the man you needed to be "out there" where the war was (didn't the magazines and movies say so? the daily papers and the pulpit?); but already it was my work which stood steady when the world rocked. I had scarcely picked up my pen when it began to replace my penis in everyone's affections. It wasn't fair. Culp, a man I at first found amusing, and brash as a bush on a hill of dung, claimed he went to work solely to summon the strength, simply to find the courage (he said), only to gain the time (he would insist) to close the clasp on his briefcase and go home. O to grow the guts! It's like leaving a full glass, he would say, staring like a lover at his desk. Although (the *I*'s rolled as though he were bowling) . . . although I am naturally capable of living without children or chatter or contretemps for long periods, I deliberately dull the memory, he always said; I put my mind's eye out; I promise myself there'll be peace, there'll be plenty, at eleven twenty-two Liane Lane, my little mortgaged lean-to, my cottage at Lake Concrete; and by god such sanctimonious self-deceptions work until I see it sitting like a sick chicken in a mud-yard, till I hear my driveway gravel crunch like dry cereal under my wheels, till I put my key in that stiff marital lock again.

I understood Culp's attitude. The office hound was a common enough creature. But like cancer, I wasn't going to contract it. Like auto accidents, it was something which broke the legs of other people. At home (he sighs like a whistle) I sit in my easy and read the Wanteds. It's my pornography. I dream of all the jobs I might be doing which would take me off, out, up, and away; I'd be Peter Pan if they paid me peanuts; and when hunger becomes overwhelming, I assuage it by chewing on checkbooks till the bills taste paid.

It wasn't fair. Martha slept like a plant, her senses all drawn in, at rest within her like a rug; while I marched into my sleeplessness as if it were a desert I was crossing (at the head of a column of sweaty and mutinous men); but the pain I felt was neither dry nor hot, but rather like a winter which will not release its grip—long gray rains raining coldly into May.

Our neighbors became our single subject. Their sounds composed a text we grew rabbinical about. From the slow sizzle of fat in a frying pan we inferred not the bacon but the pig, and their various treads upon the stairs drew a map of their marital emotions like those one gets from friends to find their cottage at the lake. (Deception. Lost ways. I knew that.) As for our own life: we cared only for concealment, nor could I burble at Marty's breasts as in the old days, or let an erection chase her through the house like a toy spear; and since our quietness kept our movements hidden, we would inadvertently sneak up on one another (sometimes Marty would shriek—it was hide and seek—when I came upon her suddenly). There was a time when our startles seemed funny. Then we would glare at the offending wall and grin at each other; but eventually the tide of attention turned, and we could only smirk at some empty corner of the ceiling and sneer at ourselves instead.

We were two pairs of turtledoves—linked by leases not by flesh, thank god!—but they were our Siamese twin, nevertheless, the mocking shadow of our sensuality; and we had scarcely reached our car in the morning when the examination of their habits began: we were outraged, amused; we giggled like girls; we had nasty arguments on points of interpretation; we considered confusing them with a barrage of false sounds, by launching attacks of heavy breathing; I suggested some interesting scenarios, but Martha would not fall in with them. We tended to take sides, Martha preferring the trail the male left, naturally—spores whose righteous quality escaped me altogether. My trust twisted to suspicion. Perhaps she was already their accomplice; perhaps she heard their passion more eagerly than she felt mine. Was the other side of the wall growing greener grass, I asked her, exasperation once more showing in my prose. Without receiving a squeak for an answer, I dropped Marty off at the local historical museum where she'd got a job minding tomahawks, propping stuffed squirrels in attitudes of life on branch-resembling sticks, and dusting flints.

The only plus was the pleasure we both took in discussing our odd and often silly circumstances with the many acquaintances we were making at the university then; and we naturally lingered over the more scandalous details, describing the pressures of so public a private life on souls as newly glued by lust and law as we were. A little untoward heat (we said) might melt us down from one another like a custard from its coating; a sudden jar might shatter our fragile ties; an un-expected stress might stretch our sympathies to a point beyond elastic (so we went on, piling comparisons up like fruit in a market window); we might weaken like moistened cardboard and our bottom pop. So our misery became entertainment like stories of the war, and from what had been a heap of jagged shards we shaped a graceful vase— something slightly salacious in the lush red-figured style. We guessed, and guessed again, and guessed some more, enlarging on our in-formation like any secret service until facts were so larded with con-jecture it became impossible to distinguish the marbling from the meat.

We were thought to be amusing—fresh, unique—(I *do* believe that)—and we certainly didn't hesitate to extricate whatever criticism of my powerful employer—our poor absent landlord—was implicit in our histories, but held it up for view and comment like a hair found floating in the soup, comparing the ironies of our situation to the slice of lemon which lies beside the cup of life; and these gibes provided an additional pleasure for our listeners, as it turned out, since the univer-sity was thought to be composed of three strata at that time—deans, dissidents, and dunces—with no one we met admitting to either ambi-tion or stupidity; so we went wild; we put grotesques in every role as real as any real ones, bringing them forth as Dickens might have done—through tubas—each with traits as neatly cubed, distinct, and freshly baked, as cakes on a plate of cakes.

My student days kept step as I marched away into marriage, the military, and my profession. College had been a long and boring banquet whose food I'd somehow digested yet couldn't excrete. There were those hierarchies and ordered rows around me still like the hedges of a labyrinth; a tropical torrent of judgments, of ranks and scores, fell without fertility; the division of days into periods of improvement, hours of regulated relaxation, a few moments of pleasure paid for by pitiless stretches of melancholy which ceased only in beery sleep, went on incessantly like the little clicks of a pedometer; for what was the distance from Martha to masturbation when you put an interior tape to it? . . . yes, there was, in particular, life at close quarters.

The memory of those makeshift apartments in Urbana followed me now like a homeless animal. I could see again the rooms which greed had eaten out of attics like moths, coal cellars covered in oil cloth like the inside of a cheap coffin, the paneled garages smelling of grease; I reoccupied those stools under dormers which made you double-up to shit, closets where the clothes-rod was a water pipe; and I remembered a friend who had an entry straddled by a shower stall, another whose bed backed against a boiler; but I particularly could not drive away the image of those tiny pre-used Polish toilets which were as close to the living room as a lamp to its chair, so that we couldn't help hear the gush of the girls, always good for a giggle, and had to aim our stream against the quiet porcelain to be discreet ourselves, or pinch it painfully thin.

I saw that Martha suffered far more than I from our unaccustomed closeness. Women weren't used to long lines of nakedness as soldiers are, or the sycamores in winter. Gaunt, bleached, boney, the trees seemed a cold growth of the snow itself, a solidification of melting air the way icicles were a congealed product of the sun.

I also recalled squatting in a cold hole once on perimeter patrol, listening with the same intensity for the enemy (and since I didn't know what the enemy would sound like, I made it up out of movies: the crunch of a boot in the snow, a frightened wheeze, the unmistakable clink of metal), my ears like those dishes they tune to the stars. The world was cemetery still, and dark as the dead beneath the stones.

Now silence was a great white field which Martha and I fled over like lines of running ink.

The trouble was, when I thought about it, that we were always the butts on the body of our anecdotes—the goats, the fall guys—the grotesques who were so amusing. And then it occurred to me to wonder whether they weren't telling tales, too, over there in biology, among faculty members we never met; and the thought was terribly sobering somehow, as if our plight were a program like Fibber Magee's that no one would want to miss; except there were two versions, two lines of listening, the right line and the left, like lobes of the brain or parties in politics; and which one was funnier, I had to speculate, which one's butts were bigger, in which did the fall guys prat more convincingly, the goats smell raunchier?

And Martha, who was always so saving, wanted to go out all the time to bars and movies, to drop in on friends where, after the customary inquiries about health and children, the rigamarole would begin again. Since we had no privacy in private, we sought it out in public. The strategy didn't succeed for either of us. Though alone in a movie with a gray screen dancing, she would throw my hand away, when it crept into hers, like a used up Kleenex, because we were married now and had, she said, no need to grope or fondle. In bars we would back ourselves in booths and speak, when we did, like conspirators. People will think we're married, all right, she said; married— but to other people. Isn't it getting to be that way (this was the general form of my reply); at home, don't you listen more to that other guy?

The cash we were conserving slipped away like our affections, literally through our fingers, as our touch became callous and mechanical. Martha grew testy about the money because she was the one who was spending it; and she grew testy about the loss of affection, because she had stopped bringing me up and never would bother again, as if her own large beauty should henceforth be enough; and though it was enough, her attitude made me resent every erection, and dislike the effect her nakedness had on me. What if all that blood became noisy, I said. What if I whistled through it like their kettle? What if, she said. What if?

In the early fall I had already begun to go down to the river to see the face of winter in the water, the slow logs and dry shoals. Crickets and hoppers were still rising ahead of my feet like miniature quail, and the weeds which had bearded the banks during the long stand of summer were high and heavily in seed; but the water returned their image to a sky which was as quiet as the river. My own face, too, fell open in the middle like the habit of a book, and by looking down, I could watch myself staring up, eyes already a bit puffy, the coming winter in my face. It was a smooth look, like an oiled door.

Here it was, our first winter, and we should have been rolled around one another like rugs. We should have been able to overcome small obstacles such as walls which were too flimsy to hold up, hide, or impede anything—which were not obstacles at all—yet here we were, our love cut judiciously in two like the front yard. How thin the skin, yet how small the poor theory that gets through, I thought, a proverb showing in my prose, a pun in my proverb like a worm. This nonsense of ours was using up my life and there was nothing I could do about it. Then I wondered whether she wasn't ashamed of me, ashamed to be heard with me in public, as though I whinnied. Would she lead a frank and noisy life with a brawny stud? Would she giggle and scream and writhe when they made love; compel that other couple to wish for pleasures they were inadequately equipped for and could not achieve even through installment dreaming?

He was tall and very thin and very dark. She was petite. She skittered, but his tread was erratic as one might imagine a scarecrow's to be—with unskillful and unfeeling feet. Mine was regular as meter (I *did* believe that), and Martha's was . . . Martha's was that of a thousand pound thistle. She put on bras and slips and blouses and sweaters, then added blazers and heavy wraps on top of that— overclothes to cover my eyes. Do you want to disappear entirely, to be snowed under layers of skirts, smocks, and mufflers? Instead, it was I who disappeared like a magician's assistant. I knew she waited until I left the house to remove her diaphragm, a smelly elastic device that no longer went in as automatically as change in a purse or keys tossed in a drawer, and would never replace the ear as an organ. I said you're making me into a stranger. Her nose peered between the tan slats of a Venetian blind she opened with scissored fingers. Our neighbor's Plymouth was, or was not, parked behind us. She felt grubby, she said. I received no requests to do her back. The museum, she complained. Dusty work. Scaly scalp. She washed always behind the bathroom door with washcloths moistened with mineral oil; dusted the davenport with damp rags; did the dishes at dawn; read in a dim light. She could slither from street dress to housecoat to nightgown without allowing a fellow a peek's worth, as one always imagined the bride of a Bedouin to be able, or a girl scout under a blanket—a skill I hadn't counted on. No one phoned. The brush man did not knock. She said it's late. What you couldn't see, perhaps you couldn't hear. I could hear a fork strike an empty plate.

The first snowfall that year caught the trees with their leaves still clinging to them, and the weight of the wet snow did what the wind hadn't—pulled them free to settle on the surface of the river. There, for a few moments at least, they resembled massive, slowly moving floes. It was a vagrant similarity, but it sucked me up from Indiana the way Dorothy was inhaled out of Kansas, placing me in an airplane near the pole where I could see below me the rocking gray water and great herds of icebergs seeking their death down the roll of the globe.

This sudden switch of vision was indeed like a light, and gave me some understanding of the actual causes of our absurd situation. We were living in an image, not in a flimsy wartime throw-up. There was no longer any reality to the clatter of pans and dishes, shoefall, outburst, sigh of a cushion; there was no world around our weary ears, only meaning; we were being stifled by significance; everything was speech; and we listened as the house talked only in order to talk ourselves, to create a saving anecdote from our oppression, a Jewish character, a Jewish joke.

Walking along the edge of the river, I no longer saw those lovely pale leaves pass me like petals, as if some river flower were blooming oddly out of season (poetry appearing abruptly in my social prose); rather I took them to be elements of a threatening metaphor, because I had suddenly seen that the world was held together only by frost and by freezing, by contraction, that its bowels contained huge compressors and ice cold molds; so the place where I stood looking over a trivial Indiana landscape—snow freshly falling upon an otherwise turgid, uninteresting stream—was actually a point on the hazardous brink of Being (and in the same sorry condition as the word, too: a seedy hotel along an Atlantic boardwalk, housing its meanings like pensioners, and by its up-steps a bent sign saying AAA); consequently there appeared before me an emblem of all that was—all that was like a frozen fog—exhaust from the engines of entropy; and I saw in the whitened leaves floating by me an honesty normally missing from Nature's speech, because this adventitious coating threw open the heart of the Law: this scene of desolation—relieved only by the barren purity of the trees—this wedge was all there was; and then I understood that the soft lull of August water was but a blanket on a snow bank; the dust that a wave of wind would raise was merely the ash of a dry summer blizzard; the daffodils which would ring our Chinese elm were blooming spikes of ice, encased in green like a thug's gloves; there was just one season; and when the cottonwoods released their seeds, I would see smoke from the soul of the cold cross the river on the wind to snag in the hawthornes and perish in their grip like every love.

Uninterpreted, our neighbor's noises were harmless, and soon would have been as dim in our consciousness as the steady eeeeeen of an electric clock, or the slow glow of a nightlight; as it was, the creak of a spring signified a body on the bed; a body, a bed—that meant fornication, transports of passion as long as a line of lorries, the free use of another for the pleasure of the self, the power to produce forgetfulness, ease, peace, sleep; it meant a disturbing measure now lay alongside our own love like a meter bar—how long? how large? how full? how deep? how final and sufficient? how useful? wise? how cheap?—and in virtue of such steps our minds had moved the whole arc of the dial, from unpremeditated act to accidental sound, from accidental sound to signal, from signal to sense, from sense to system, from system to . . . the chaos implicit in any complete account.

For a month we fell toward the ice at the center of hell (grandeur finally showing in my prose), and I think it was the weather which convinced us we were bored and beaten by surveillance; we were at last embarrassed by the bloated selves our stories had made of us; close quarters had become half dollars, although, in this small pocket, we jangled together without real change. But now the wind came up the river like a steamer. The windows iced over. Would pipes freeze? I called responsible people and received assurances which didn't assure me. We told our friends of these fresh troubles, but I felt none of their former warm interest. We had worn the rug until I couldn't read its welcome. The center was gone. Only 'we/me' remained beneath the shuffle of our feet. So we struggled into English sweaters and wore wool socks; we went to movies to replace our feelings, and sat in bars to keep warm and lose touch. With malice in my symbolism, I drank boilermakers—to lose track, I said, without a smile to greet the pun— and on placemats which displayed a map of the campus the color and shape of a spilled drink, I wrote to friends about positions in the south.

Culp was the only exception. He retold our stories for us, harboring our grudges until they seemed the flagships of his own fleet. He became another kind of auditor, his intense interest hemming us in on what we might otherwise have thought was our free and open elbow—the out side. Perhaps it was Culp who had worn our welcome thin, for he would show up at parties, picnics, and processions, to chortle and nudge, allude and remind, elaborating on our originals until they began to shrink within the convoluted enclosures he gave them the way paintings dwindle inside heavy ornate frames, or turtles hide. That predatory historian, Martha fumed, has kidnapped our life; and she was right, but not for ransom, as I still believe; Culp holds whole booths of convention bars enthralled with reminiscences of those difficult early years of his marriage, when he lived in a hut on the banks of the Wabash (a double-hovel, he already called it), encountering everywhere in his own air the image of another, as of course he said, like finding someone else's fart in your own pants.

How are you, I'd ask Martha with real worry. How are you feeling? Of course I was concerned for my own safety. I wanted to know if a storm was coming. It sometimes seemed to me I could see snow sliding out of the ceiling and melting on us as it melted on the river, though now the river was beginning to freeze, to disguise the flow of its feeling beneath a shell of ice. The sycamores were stoic, and there were deep crusted holes in the drifts where I'd walk. I found my tracks a comfort. Where I had been I would be again, returning to old holes, yet they were only the weather's memory. I wondered whether this winter's warfare would disappear in the spring, or would we be mired down in mud like the troops in Flanders?

We'll look for another place, I promised. What's in the fine print? Perhaps we can break our lease; maybe keep a big flea-barking dog. Martha's enthusiasm was persuasively unconvincing. Perhaps she didn't want to be alone with me again. Did she sense what was surfacing? Maybe she liked the protection. Say, I said, suppose I turned vicious, you'd be safe. One peep would be as good as calling police. Martha mimed a scream, her mouth so wide it could have swallowed a fist. Oh no, even if you were murdering me, they wouldn't murmur, she said—would we murmur? We might shout "shut up!" like they do in the big city movies; we might bang on pipes the way you do to call the super; we might return outcries like party invitations. Martha shrugged. Her cleavage was another cunt. Well, I might do any one of those things, I suppose, she said; I think they're in my nature; but not you—oh no, not you, ever. It would be impolite and forward and beneath your blessed dignity. Then why am I staring at the floor like a schoolboy? The gods look down, don't forget, she said. Our floors were made of that hard asphalt tile which broke your feet (I had dubbed the color "abattoir brown" when we'd first moved in), and that's what I saw when I hung my head: the frozen bleeding feet of every piece of furniture which had stood there through the war, leaving their pitiful dents, as if the scars were records of wounds in the weights which made them; and of course that was it, the world was tipping toward the north, relations were in deep reverse, blooms invading their buds, snow rising like steam from the earth, as in this doubled house, where stoves seemed warmed by their pots and compliments were a curse; for now when I entered my pale, silent, snowed-over wife, given legally to me by family, god, and social custom, it was through a cunt which lit up like an exit, and I was gone before I arrived.

The gods, I said. Marty? the gods? You speak of the gods to someone who was never a choirboy. I'm sort of lonely little gid who looks into his shoes for a sight of the stars.

I had wanted to be put in charge of her body, not exactly as though she were a platoon, but as though my soul would wear her flesh for a change, and I would look out for her elbows as though they were my own, eat well and not take cold; but she wouldn't play. I remembered kids like that when I was a kid. They wouldn't be the baby or the pupil or the robber or the renegade; they wouldn't lie still like the sick or wounded; they would never fetch, seek out, or serve. They were too afraid. I'm not a train, Whiffie, and I don't need a conductor. You mean you're not a plane, and you don't need a pilot. I'm not a boat and don't need a skipper. I'm not a field that needs a tractor. I hate those images. I'm a daughter, but I *have* a father.

She could have had my body in exchange, but who wants to be the boss of a barnyard, the cock for such a nervous vane? Speaking of images, Marty, how's the one you are living in presently; the one that's made you the thunder sheet in the sound-room, a roof in a heavy rain? But it was no use. She no longer cared for what I cared for. Henceforth she'd let her body burgeon like a lima bean in a Dixie cup, though there were no kids, yet, to instruct or entertain. If she had deeded it to me; if she . . . well, both of us would be as trim now as the mold of a painted window.

Surely we haven't gone so fast in these few weeks we've passed middle age in our marriage? Is it the sound barrier we've broken, and are they the boom, now, we're supposed to hear? It makes no sense. It makes at least one, she always answered, even when we were courting, because the statement was a tic of mine, like that obnoxious nasal sniff I had, she said. As a matter of fact, Marty darling, we've grown as sluggish as a pair of snakes, and if any such barrier burst, it would have to happen from the slow side of swift, like your hymen, remember? I said, letting my prose grow unshavenly toward scratch. In this house sound certainly departs for all points like the humans of Hiroshima, she said, serene and uninsulted. Sometimes I think that's all they are over there—echoes of us—that whole half of the house is an echo, a later ring of our present life, and it's me, then, I hear, going up their stairs.

On *her* feet? that scatter of pins?

Save your jokes for the next show, Whiff. She smiled with a meanness I hadn't seen. And she had begun to braid her hair again, a bad sign, and write long letters to her mother—one a day, like pills. Oh no, Koh, not on *her* pins, on *his* needles, she said. Martha stared at our barely wrappered wall for a moment so pointedly I thought there might be a gap through which she saw a table or a teapot more substantial than the shadows of our own. What are his shoes, anyway, but the sound of my steps? You'll find my feet fastened beneath those almost negligible legs and skinny trunk next time you meet.

No such luck, Marty. Clutching groceries or garbage like a pair of paper bellies, what else do we embrace? In any case, we never see a shoe.

You've heard that small black head of his, haven't you? like a photographer's box, go click? She laughed but I never understood the cause. The pleasure it implied seemed out of place. He's a thorough look-see sort of man—complete—including that long lank hair which shuts out the light; and there's his dark transparent face as well, like exposed film you can safely see the sun through at the noon of an eclipse.

Martha did nothing to erase the extravagance of her description. A luksi sort of man, I thought. Of the monkeys, that's not the one I would have picked; but I must admit to receiving a chill from this news—a chill, a chill—though in a perverse way it restored my weakened self to life like a dead drink that's suddenly got a plop of fresh ice.

The silences which came between us now were as regular as spaces on a page of type, and far more impervious to any message than our walls.

You called yourself a gid. That must be good. So what's a gid? She hated to ask. She knew how I loved an answer.

A gid is a small god, Marty, the human kind, with more features than powers—the difference, you might say, between poetry and prose. With my fingers I made a meager measure. Mayor Daley is a gid. And Franco. Fred Astaire. Lowell Thomas.

Then you're not a gid. Do they come in smaller sizes like bras?

I hated her when she was smart-assing. A gid is as small as gods get. There's no volume for a vowel deeper down or deeper in.

She wondered whether it came from 'giddyup' or 'yid' or simply 'giddy,' and then scornfully concluded it wasn't a word, that I'd merely made it up. We argued wearily about whether a made-up word could be one, and whether making up words was a form of lying, though neither of us cared. Well, in any case, you're not a gid, she said. I hated her when she was hard-boiling. I hated her when she crossed her arms across her chest like a prison matron in the movies. Her cleavage was another cunt. Hey, why don't we? why don't we invite them to dinner? Perhaps we can reach an understanding. Maybe we can work something out.

I don't want to know him any better than I do already, Martha said, carrying a summer *Vogue* into the john.

I was resolutely bent on comedy. If we could trade one-liners maybe we could continue to live. I suggested we let our little throw-rugs grow so we could comb them across our cold bald floors.

It may be, Martha said distantly.

I began to wish I had the wind's indifference to what it did. Shall I water them then? I tried to shout. Her first flush filled both houses like the bowl. There were always two. But she had begun to hide her habits from me. She kept the corners of her toast out of her coffee; she didn't twist her table napkin; she no longer whistled while doing crosswords, or used toilet paper to blow her nose. She started rubbing toothpaste on her gums with her right forefinger, and thrusting pencils between her braids. She didn't dog-ear books; she kept caps firmly on her jars of cleansing cream; she stopped slapping around the house in scuffs. I was simply at a loss. She didn't stick her lips anymore, but that might have been fashion. I waited for that second flush which didn't come. She was disguising herself. Her voice would get gruff. Soon I could expect to see a stranger's expression on her face and a mask on her muff.

With even these petty expectations taken from me, all I had left was a little inner determination, gid-greed, ambition like a stunted bud; but I silently resolved that what Ike is, and Cotton Mather was, Whiffie Koh would be.

We lit electric fires but no others. Except for them our house was a cold grate, and we were as alive as sifting ash. Peeled outside-in by Marty's transformations—bewildered, shocked—I only professed to be surprised so she would believe I always knew. But knew what? Was my blond Martha taking on that little woman's ways? The joke became our medium of exchange.

We would drive them out like demons. I made the sign of the cross—incorrectly—and muttered Latin imprecations. Let's burn sulphur, I said. For a week I tried raising my voice and being rowdy. Martha read old *Cosmos* and did puzzles ripped from the *Saturday Review.* It's like living in a waiting room, she said. And hearing you bawl about like someone calling trains.

That's it, I said. If I took a snapshot of our life right now, what would it look like? yeah, a drawing, a cartoon. We've bound our own feelings like feet. Our cheeks have porked. My eyes are two dots. Everything we say belongs in a balloon. Listen to your own sweet voice: stars, contorted ampersands, and yellow lightning bolts. Marty, these last few weeks I've felt myself emptying into outline, as if beer could become its bottle, and because we're posed here in pitchfork, arrowed tail, and red flesh, how can our misery be any more than lines? Hey, remember how we honeyed one another? Has so much changed we've gathered only ants and flies? Marty? listen—

Lis-sen, she said. That's all I do. My left ear is as long and flat as this wall I've pressed it to so amorously, and I've kept the other to the ground as well, just as hard and down and often, so the right one here is wide and tired and dirty like the floor. My nose, Koh, in case you care, gets nothing up a nostril now but doorbell buzz and blender whirr.

So we turned up the radio to stifle our whispers and smother our shouts, as torturers did in the movies, but discovered that then we couldn't hear anything they were up to either, and that wouldn't do.

The entire house seemed to have shrunk. It had become a cheerless, shabby rented room, soon to be a bureau drawer. I had been about to suggest that we stop bugging one another, but a dreary cold light fell out of the kitchen to confound me, and my voice lay down in my throat.

The other day I saw a fire alarm—long yellow streaks like slaps across the face of the street. I've three bruises on my arm. It's the vicious way he turns off taps. Notice that? They roll marbles across their kitchen floor. He leans over her like a lens.

Marty, come on. It's our closeness in this crazy place—our closeness has kept us apart—but the natural, decent, and sensible thing to do would be to complain to the university together—club up, unionize, make common cause. We *have* a common cause, you know.

She acknowledged this by gestures, each Italian and obscene. Remember how those woppy Eyetie kids would gun their Vespas through the streets? the noise came at you as though they were hurling the cobbles. Well, they loved it. They loved their loud cocks. They loved their ball-like wheels. They loved to stick it up those narrow Roman ways. A vigorous finger speared the air. She failed to strip skin from her teeth. Can't you hear them next door, then? that continuous applause? the cheers? They love it—this noise we volley. They wouldn't trade for Willie Mays.

I hated her when she was hard-assing. I hated her when her plump face resembled that of some mean and pouty child, as—so often—it resembled Charles Laughton's. But, Marty, it can't really be that only our half of the house is cold. Noise isn't a trolley on a one-way *Milano* street. It can't be that moisture is collecting on our sills and not theirs, or that just our drafts are so brisk the blinds rise and the drapes wave.

It may be, Martha said. What if?

You know, Whiff, sometimes, in a marriage, only one side hears the other cough.

Yeah? Well. What of it? Are we married to them, then? Is that the situation?

One side is cold, sometimes, in a marriage, she said. One *eye* does all the weeping.

Yeah. Right. Sure thing. But is our nose stuck in their mouldy jam pot? And who is the cold carrot around here anyhow? which side of our bed has a marble mattress?

Shush, she said. They've just come in.

Shit, I shouted, on the run; but no sound could give me satisfaction, nor the silence after my slam.

The bitterness of it. I had hoped her flesh might warm my life; but my body isn't blubber for your burning, she had crudely said. Alas, one's dreams are always a cliché, yet I had hoped she would fill what I felt was an emptiness; but I'm not going to let you wear me like a padded bra so you can seem complete, she said.

The wind was an acid eating at my face, my anger another sort of acid searing my insides. Soon they would be near enough to greet. There was a hint of starlight, as there often was during the many clear nights of this pitiless winter, the thin moon a menacing sickle, and the dark vein of the river ran through closing ice toward a heart far out of sight, I imagined, like a lurking troll beneath a bridge. I couldn't drive her from her fantasies, however I tried. She was persistent as a bee. My boots went again where my boots had been, and I was aware, without pleasure, of the repetition. What was my passion for this ample woman but just that amplitude, that generous expanse of self? and now her hair was coiled, her thighs tense, her feelings like a tissue wadded in an anxious hand.

We went from apology to explanation to excuse like partners at a progressive dinner.

It bothers me to be an object in other people's obscenities, she said—the dirt in a dirty joke—a filthy thought you can't wash clean or even get a little soap near.

Even in *my* polite pornographies, I asked, with another attempt at gaiety which would burst before blowing up like a bad balloon.

In yours, especially, now I've been *his* leading lady. Her head wagged toward the wall in a gesture of such furious rejection I became immediately jealous. It bothers me to be all crotch. It bothers me.

And so I thoughtlessly said I wouldn't mind being all prick, dropping my left like an amateur, exposing myself; and of course I received her swift, professional retort. Replies rose in my throat, but they had the quality of yesterday's radish, so I did not return her pings with any pong of mine. I don't see even a shadow to start at, let alone a reality to run from, I said; how can you know what either of them is thinking?

I know what *I* am thinking. I know what *my* thoughts watch. I know how he drinks his morning milk. I have the measure of his moustache, and how far along his lip his tongue creeps. I know what he sees in his wife. I know how he pees, and when he shits, how many squares of paper are pulled off. I hear the rattle of the roll. I know what he wants.

My anger would never leave me. I had contracted a malarial disease. Naturally I had to hear what she imagined our neighbor saw in his wife, and Martha answered, predictably: the same things you see in me—our sentences two halves of the same dull bell. A hammer, I said, is what I see. A pliers. God damn it, Marty, don't cheat on the truth so transparently. Do you want a use? the least utility? Just what do you believe I see when I see inside you? the peep show follies?

Hair and heat and pink toes. You see a plate of steaming meat.

I wished right then there were a god I could invoke to damn her truly, but the thought of her skin cracking open in some supreme heat gave me only a jack-off's relief. Of course I shouldn't have felt as if my soul had left me, but her words—common enough, really—were like that winter wind which rushes by so fast you can't get a bite of it for breathing.

Not quite, Marty, I said. When I look at you I see a stew congealing in its grease.

The bitch didn't even weep.

The bitterness of it. I could remember her body in its beauty waiting for me with the calmness of the coverlet. I, too, had looked at her like a lens, and she had posed for me, opened as easily as eyes to my eyes; showed a boisterous bust, a frank and honest hip, a candid cunt, as one might hand round snapshots of a trip. Then it struck me. Perhaps she believed, in those handsome early days when our lust was in its clean beginnings and the politics of the penis had not yet confused and corrupted everything, that I was gazing past her smooth full cheeks and succulent lobes toward Martha the grandly scutcheoned Muhlenberg I'd married, or grazing quite beyond her meadowed chest to Marty the blond Amazonian lass, so she didn't mind my meddling senses, my nosey fingers, my tireless tongue; whereas now she knew I was admiring nothing but her beauty right along; and though it might be, like wealth, of immense use, it remained an alien and external burden if you thought of adding it to the self, because—well—she believed she possessed her looks like one might a Pekinese or poodle, and who would want to incorporate a cold-nose, pissy-nervous, yapping one of those? yes, wasn't that it? for hadn't I always wondered that very thing about women, whom I had learned could be sensuous and passionate beyond my poor capacities; who could calculate faster than Clever Hans—cook, sing, farm, run households, wag ass and empire with equal ease and often with the same moves, betray causes, author novels, and learn French—but in whom I had never seen, for instance, what a sculptor must, namely how dirty the mind gets where it feeds like a root in the earth, or the extraordinary way the concrete is composed of numbers and relationships like sand, the fugal forms of feeling which outstrip all proof, or finally the snowy mountainous elevations, the clouded unscaled peaks, the cold remote passions of the purely physical sublime?

You don't get it, do you, Martha said. You think I'm being cranky and perverse. You think I should be locked up like a dirty line in a limerick. Koh. You dear love. You runt. You dunce. She smiled to lower the level of her malice, but there was still enough to wet my hair. I went to the bathroom a moment ago, she said. First I heard my own feet, you know? I heard the click of the light switch, the snick of the latch, the rubbered settle of the seat. It shames me to think that someone else may hear what I just heard, what I just made—the splash of my pee, that lovely shush of bubbles like soda dying in its glass—because these are my sounds, almost internal to me, Koh, the minor music of my privacy, and to hear them is to put a hand on me in a very personal place.

I heard the same snick, I said. It signals your safety, doesn't it? as if I might burst in behind you to piss between your legs myself.

Oh Koh. Please. It's not simply that my noises might be embarrassing—a rumbling stomach or some raucous break of wind—or even that to hear them one would have to be a sneak—although such factors weigh . . . they weigh . . . but neither is the painful one, the last cruel twist which wrings me out.

Slowly seeping down like egg white on a wall: my depression was that desperate. A kitchen table grainy with crumbs, an ashtray heaped with butts like the burned-out bodies of our voided thoughts, a faded cushion and a shredded towel—companions for this exercise—then a light that rattled away off plates like a falling fork. And so I said: have you heard your legs lock, Marty? No snick there, no click, rather a sound like the settle of the seat.

Oh—

No O, I said. No. X. Have you seen your arms cross on your chest like a sign warning Railroad?

Koh—

And when my hands fall on your bottom, I said, not to spank, because we never enjoyed that relation, but like a corn flake, a tree seed, ever so lightly, as air through an open doorway, surely you've felt those buttock muscles tighten?

Please, Whiff. Please be serious. Please.

Seriousness, I answered, has all but overcome my prose.

I remember wanting to understand, to throw my sympathy like an arm around her shoulders (at one point I thought, "gee, she's still my girl," as if we were pinned or going steady and I was selfishly rushing her responses); but I was also angry, disappointed, deeply affronted (I began to believe we wouldn't last the year out), since here she was defending her bloomers before I'd fully got her skirt up, and I was bitter as though bereft, because the cause of her present sensitivity seemed just a case of damn bad luck like getting flashed by the cops while making out in Lovers' Lane, and had nothing to do, inherently, with us as a couple. My outrage rapidly became metaphysical. I called down on all women the character of my mother like a plague, and then cursed them with her fate.

You know that passage in *Middlemarch*—

I knew no passage in *Middlemarch*, but I can recall insisting that it was *every* female's favorite fiction.

—where she says about marriage that there's something awful in the nearness it brings?

I was sitting in a sugar maple chair the sticky color of its syrup. I was uncomfortably near the knobs on metal cabinets, size of my eyes. Martha was wearing a large floral print which made her look like a trellis. To my well-fed Marty, I was a bed and boarding party. Wise-cracks, rhymes, lay discarded like the Sunday paper. At such close quarters, our war was now down to nickels and dimes.

I've been watching us together, Koh, and I've been thinking, too, of our twins over there like animals in a neighboring cage, and I'm convinced now that we need to live in at least the illusion that a certain important portion of our life passes unobserved; that there are walks we take which leave no tracks; acts whose following sounds are not broadcast like the bark of dogs; events to which no one need or should respond; which have, in effect, no sensuous consequences.

I wished that this were one of them, but a metal kettle and a kitchen stool threatened immediate animation—to dance à la Disney to a tune by Dukas. The cute I couldn't handle. The spout would say something like "Toot!"

I don't want to hear all I do—every squeak in my works. I want a bit of oblivion, Koh. I want a little rest from awareness. You've made me so conscious of my chest, I'm counting breaths.

I was rolling like a spool. There's no coughless cold, kiddo; no blow without a little snot, no ding without its answering ling, no—

How I hate it when you try to crack wise. You can't break clean. You mash. Sure, sneer. Never mind. You can't ride away on the back of a joke. That's what I'd like to do myself, though: become deaf to what's dumb. Grin. Go ahead. How I hate it when you put that smile on like a dirty sock. Whiff, I'm sick of the shimmy, jounce, and rattle of staying alive. I want a world for a while without echoes and shadows and mirrors, without multiples of my presence. I could cut off my silhouette and not cry.

You're a sweet one to want a smooth ride. I thought you liked life a little hump-woof-and-rumpy.

Well, Willie, at least you offer me a model, a measure, something to go by when I wonder in what way you love me: exactly like a marksman loves his bull's-eye. All you want to do is score.

She spread the slats to check for their car, facing her sweatered back to my dismay.

On our own, she said softly. Left alone . . . in time . . . to some things we can go mercifully blind, as our ears will grow swiftly indifferent, thank god, and all our other senses . . . indifferent to ourselves and the cells we calendar our days in.

Above the sink the lamp sang, and the small chain leaked from its harsh fluorescent light in little links like melting ice.

Remember when my mother had her asshole out, Marty said (she knew how I hated her coarseness, but she was an *aficionado* of my shame); remember how she had to shit in a sack? She got used to it. She got used to it because she had to survive. She got used to it because nobody dared to remind her. The subject was delicately *dropped.*

Like those A-bombs under their umbrellas. Marty, you can't cancel the fall-out on account of rain, when it's the bloody rain itself.

What I want, Whiff—if it goes off—I want a chance to ignore the noise. Yeah, cover your ears like one of those monkeys to mock me, but I'm no longer lost in our love as I once was. I keep surfacing. I feel on film.

You don't like the lead in our little blue movies? the star part? It can't be that you're bored with the graceless grunt and huffypuffy business?

You'll laugh at me alone this time, lover. I can't keep you company. You sprawl there with your little friend crawling down your trousers waiting for me to weep so you can take it out and put it in, because quarreling makes it uncaring, hence stiff and amorous like the little toy soldier it is. Go on. Take it off somewhere on vacation. Run away to the river. Amuse the ice. The two of you can take a leak, have a good laugh with the snow and the weeds.

I did as I was told, throwing on my coat as though I were throwing off everything else. The sky was hard and brilliant with stars like a run of the right hand in a piece by Liszt. The cold air rinsed my lungs and gave them definition. All those hidden inner organs took my walk and lived no differently than I did. Even our porous duplex didn't overstep its bounds. Beneath my weight, the cold snow crushed like crisp paper in a fist.

With Martha I loved what I'd always loved: an outline, a surface, a shape—yes—a nipple, a lip; yet I'd become an alien in her household, an unwanted presence, worse than roaches or the wind, because she thought she was more than a football, a weight, a slack wet mouth or sack of warm skin, when no one was other than their image, print, and circumcision—none of us—we were nothing but a few rips in the general stuff of things like rust on a nickel blade, and we were each running down like radium into rays.

So I was the thin dark man next door now, not the fair round pudge she'd married. I was the swiveling radar dish, the probe, the lens, the receiver of all her transmissions. Still, it would have been useless to remind her that a dog could smell the absence of her clothes, so she'd be naked to it, though they were walls away, since she was contemptuous of my philosophizing, which she'd called mental masturbation more than once; yet if we conceived the world properly, we would realize the birds, ants, and insects also know us this way: as a shadow, a sound, a scent, a sudden intrusive substance, a cutting edge—never as a soul which (please god) does not exist except in a moist cold cloud like my present breath; and that, however quiet we were, however much we muffled our oars and stoppered our mouths, little could be kept from the earth and air around us, lion our lives upwind as we'd like, because it was alive as an antelope, all ear and apprehension, anticipation and alarm.

I was too much the whole of that wide world. Yes. I sniffed you out wherever you went like a hound. I would rush from another room to say: you coughed, is everything ok? but for you that was spying, not concern; so when I rubbed your rump I did so only to molest you; and when I offered to comb your hair you wondered what was up, and jeered when you saw what was. You wanted a love which would have been a lie—to lie beyond the nostril and the hip—an imaginary island like Atlantis or those happy beaches of the blessed it cost them nothing to enjoy beyond the payment of their death.

The mouth was refused first, before her back was turned like the last page. What are we, Marty, but sense and inference? and when I feel your smooth warm skin, your breasts like playful puddles; when I nuzzle your underarms or scent the ultimate *nostos* of your nest; what do I infer from what I sense? surely not the brittle stick you've thrown me. Be large, I begged. You will be less, my love, if you give me less.

The bitterness of it. But there was, as in everything, some recompense. It was true I enjoyed the way my feet distressed the snow; and I approved the sycamores who had no pretensions and wouldn't have hid their bones from me on any account, or condemned my pleasures. I did not applaud the river for its beauty because along this stretch it had none. I loved it, rather, for its welcoming indifference, the way the cold was cold, and kept me together. What, of this world of memories, a young gent's hopes, the pale ashes of desire, could I control, or oversee, or lie in wait for like the man next door I now would always be?

It was a winter so prolonged their crocus bloomed beneath the snow, and the sun dreamed.

Out of a frozen bottle would be forced the frozen cream; and I felt my heart expand against my chest, my coat, as though squeezed, to press against the tree trunks, push against the pointed stars, spread out upon a sterile land.

We'd remain married. I would see to that. One life would not be long enough for my revenge. The coarse baritone in which I made my vows came like an errant echo from another skull, an outcry left behind on the stage like an actor's closing lines. My voice in my fist, I promised the wind, trampling underfoot my former prints, Iago now the new friend, blade, and ancient, of my prose.

Johnny Appleseed

Susan Neville

H E TOLD me that his ancestor had left his hard black seeds in neat rows where scrub pine or thistle, cockle or thorns would have grown and that when people stopped just long enough to eat the apples he had planted they felt their feet become like iron and their heads become drugged and when they tried to move, found that they, like the trees, couldn't. And in turn, he said, the people planted squash and corn and ate the apples freely, spreading more black seeds whose roots joined under the earth in dark rivers which spread under the houses which also grew from the seeds, wrapping around children's knees, strangling pipes until they had to dig more and more wells.

And he told me I was still under the spell of those trees of his ancestor and I said I didn't believe that until he said would I leave in the morning with him for Zanzibar and I said no. And he pointed to the trees behind my house, black as obsidian against the darkening sky, and he said the black branches were the rivers from the apple trees, spreading out like sap at this time of night, and that to him they were a cutout in the sky. If I looked closely I could see stars where the bark should be. I looked closely and didn't see stars, but there were stars outlined with gunmetal on the hat he wore and I liked it when he stroked his beard a certain way and I didn't care about the trees or the bark or his illusions. He said he was a direct descendant of Johnny Appleseed, that he had the same name, and that once he had even seen him in a bar in Kansas City, the original Johnny, toting glossy catalogs, posing as an undergarment salesman so he could say "negligee" and "brassiere" to the women who came in. He said that he himself was an itinerant magician, specializing in appearing and disappearing, that I'd already seen one-half of his act. He put his arms on my shoulders and asked was I anxious to see the other half and I said no, I wasn't. Then he asked again if I would leave with him for Zanzibar and I said no, but I'd put him up in the garage for the night. He said that was a trick question; since I'd said no I was in need of help and he would stay around until I said yes. I told him he sounded crazy, I thought he was just a tramp, but he pulled his beard and bent his knee slowly so that rings of cloth crawled up his leg and I thought, what could be the harm? Stay, but only for one night. By that time the cut-out trees had bled into the rest of the sky; there were stars around his head as well as on it.

I pulled a mattress into the garage while he sat crouched on a high shelf watching, hanging by rakes, shovels, hoes. His eyes the same silver gray as the gunmetal, they glinted in the dark unevenly, like crumpled tinfoil. He mumbled while I worked, eyes always on me while he mumbled. I covered the mattress with fresh sheets, sprayed lavender between, set a Chinese enameled lamp on a short table, asked him if he needed a blanket. I tried to ignore his incantations. They started low.

Johnny Johnny Johnny Johnny whoops Johnny whoops Johnny Johnny Johnny Johnny

I placed a piece of chocolate on his pillow.

whoops Johnny whoops Johnny Johnny Johnny Johnny Johnny

Sweet cream in a pitcher beside the bed.

Johnny whoops Johnny whoops Johnny Johnny Johnny

I left him in the garage. I locked the door. The bed had looked nice, like a movie set looks—complete where the light reached, but framed by dark and oil and hard metal beaks of machinery. I tried to imagine him sleeping in it.

I went into the house, opened doors and windows for air, locked screens, stopped by a window and touched the screen with my tongue. It was bitter and the taste lasted. I thought about the song I would probably go upstairs to write about a woman whose only sense was taste. About all the things she could touch with her tongue before she died a tragic death from rare infectious germs.

But when I opened the door to my room, Johnny Appleseed was there waiting, the hat with the gunmetal stars slid halfway under the bed. I asked him how he'd found his way past me. He told me that I hadn't really locked anything, that I'd allowed him to come in. I picked up the hat and put it on the dresser. He flipped open a pocketknife and took out a block of wood from between the sheets. Soon he had wood shavings all over the bed. He said the block of wood had once been a whole tree, that he made tiny smooth rings from the wood, that I would find them useful. I said if you're really Johnny Appleseed, shouldn't you have a bag of seeds? He motioned to the empty side of the bed with the blade of his knife.

I said, if you're really a magician, Johnny Appleseed, show me some tricks. He sat on a moonlit tree limb in the cemetery, carving faces in the bark, chips falling on a stone by my feet. Leaping to the ground, he moved the pocketknife toward my eyes, brandished it in the air. See the lights on the blade, he said. I'm carving chips from the moon. Catch one. I touched a reflection of the moon, buried in the hair on his chest. *Now watch the blade, Johnny Johnny Johnny. See the blade bend, Johnny, stroke it, stroke the blade.* I stroked it. The blade didn't bend. *Stroke it, Johnny Johnny,* he said. He moved my hand along the metal, *stroke the blade, watch it bend.* It's flat, I told him. His face moved closer to mine, the hard edge of his hat brushed my ear, he winked. Isn't it amazing that the blade is bending? he said. Bending to match the contour of the earth, he said. The earth is flat here, I said. It looks flat, he said, but it's really bending; it has to, you know, it has to bend everywhere. Not around here, I said. A circle bends everywhere, he said; it appears flat like the earth, but it's really bending. It's flat, I said. Very very flat.

He tossed the knife at the tree. It folded in half and fell to the ground. He turned his wrist and a wooden ring appeared in his hand, rough-hewn. I'm sure I saw it slide down your sleeve, I said. The satin shirt had rippled, I'd seen it ripple. Sit, he said. I sat on the stone amid the shavings. He slipped the ring over my foot, around my left ankle. Another turn of the wrist and another ring appeared, this one smooth sanded, varnished. He slid it over my right hand. A larger one appeared. He slid it up my right leg, around my thigh. That's enough of that, Johnny Appleseed, I said, I feel very unbalanced. He slid one up my left thigh and asked me to stand. I clacked when I tried to walk toward him. Now where's the trick, Johnny Appleseed? I said. Try to take them off, he said. I tried and they wouldn't come off, they were stuck, and I said they must have shrunk from my sitting on the ground. I said at least-clack clack-help-clack-me remove-clack clack clack-one from one thigh-clack. One of the rings slid from my leg as if it were greased. I'll figure out how to do it, I said. I know it's an illusion.

He took my hand and led me to a flat gravestone, pallid white and cold. He chanted *Johnny Johnny* and I lay down on the stone. The letters were indented deep in the rock; I could feel someone's name and dates digging into my back. He lay down, brown curls near my lips, the wooden ring burning on my thigh. Over his shoulder was the tree, its leaves silver, fruit as bright and hard as crystal marbles, cat's eye marbles in my hands, the clicking limbs. Johnny jump up, be nimble, be quick. I rolled over onto the grass. His back on the stone, he said that might be what death feels like. If it does, then it's not so bad, I said, and I brushed the wet hair back from his eyes. He said Johnny Appleseed had planted the apples because he had been afraid to leave the land to the dead things, the wild things. That his own destiny was to face them, that he was building a power, that there was no security for him. He gripped my hand and stared at the sky; it was filled with clouds and moving with a violence. I could sense that the emptiness frightened him. The cemetery was quiet. Then he threw his legs into the air in an arc, did a kip to his feet, and pulled me up with him. I fingered the ring clutching my wrist. Mirrors, I said. You must do it with trick mirrors.

He came once to watch me where I worked, coming in late after I'd finished most of my set, wearing the hat with the gunmetal stars and jeans and a muslin shirt and a floor-length apron with stenciled colored moons and seaweed on the bib. He asked for a table up front and the waitress gave it to him. He ordered a pitcher of sweet cream and ten ounces of bourbon. His table was in the light from the stage; he sat in the shadow. All I could see were his disembodied hands pouring the cream and bourbon into a glass, lifting the glass into the air and setting it down. The place I worked was decorated like a speakeasy—dim lights, waitresses in flapper costumes, pictures of gangsters on the wall. I was dressed like a moll in a red satin dress, greasy red lipstick. I carried a plastic carbine. I sang old jazz, mostly Billie Holliday and Bessie Smith, sometimes some of my own songs that I wrote to sound like that same style jazz. I was glad he'd come because it seemed to be my chance to mesmerize him. The satin dress molded my body with stripes of moving lights, clung tightly to my hips. There was a slit up the side to my waist and I wore a black leotard and black hose, though it was difficult getting the hose through the wooden ring on my thigh. My voice wasn't great, I knew, but was throaty and rich and my movements were good. Men were always coming up to me after the show, wanting to give me a ride home. I had always said no. I sat on a round table and did a turn, easy with the satin dress. I lay back on the table, legs crossed, carbine on my knee. I caressed the microphone with my finger as I sang, looking over to the table where Johnny was sitting.

> *If I should get a notion*
> *To jump right in the ocean*
> *Aint nobody's business if I do.*

I slid off the table and walked over to Johnny. I stroked his hair with the point of the carbine. It tangled in one place and I pulled it out gently. I still couldn't see his whole face, just half of it with a reddish glow from the floor lights. He was half smiling, elfin. The stars on his hat glowed red, more like planets. I walked away and did a few grinds as I sang, something I don't usually do. I walked over to the upright piano and played with the band during the riffs. I looked at Johnny's table, the glass still rising and falling as if by levitation. Suddenly his fingers began to move fast, at the same rate as mine moved on the piano keys. I looked and gold coins began to slide out from between his fingers and clatter on the table. More and more coins appeared in the air. He dropped handfuls; they formed a mound in front of him. I played more intricate riffs; we began to improvise, the band and I. Playing wilder. More coins appeared. Soon the stage manager focused an amber light on Johnny's table. The crowd thought he was part of the show and they applauded. I noticed the band was beginning to play background to him, slowing when his hands slowed, at times becoming frenetic when his hands began to blur. Birds appeared in the air, flapped around the table, tiny globes of blue lights like moons circled among the birds, cards materialized and vanished and still coins were pouring onto the table and off, clattering to the floor. Waitresses stopped bringing drinks. There were no more conversations. Just the sound of the band and the birds and Johnny's silent seductions. He picked up the pitcher of sweet cream and turned it over on the table. No liquid ran out and when he picked it up again, there was a mound of apples which rolled lopsided and thudded off the table. He squashed one beneath his heel. He reached into the air and held each bird, each coin, each moon with his hand and when he opened his hand they were gone. Then both of the hands moved suddenly, pushing the gold coins off the table. Some of them rolled toward me, landing at my feet. *Oh Johnny Johnny,* I whispered. *Oh Johnny.*

I finished my set and he was waiting by the door when I left. He winked and said, "You know where I can find any bootleg whiskey, baby?" All of that stops at this door, I told him. The illusion stops here, doesn't it? I stepped into the night air. This is real, isn't it? He turned me to face him. The apron was slung over his shoulder. His shirt was unbuttoned, the hair on his chest thick and matted. His hand slid down my satin dress, fingered the ring on my thigh. You make a good moll, he said. I put my hand in his shirt, ran up and down his side. I'm looking for cards, I said. Trick cards. You won't find them, he told me. You definitely won't find them. I felt something cold graze my ear lobe. He produced a fifty-cent piece. Come on, he said, I'll buy you a cup of coffee. I reached for the coin and it disappeared. *Oh Johnny Johnny,* I whispered again. *Oh Johnny Johnny.*

Wooden rings holding back the kitchen curtains, hanging from the ceiling like mobiles. Five wooden rings on each arm which clattered when I moved. One ring hugging my neck, rings hidden beneath tables and chairs, between the sheets on my bed, thin ones between the leaves of books, filling pans and skillets, sandwiched between slices of bread. I sealed a drawer in the kitchen shut, the drawer that contained the knives. I sealed the drawer with paraffin because the knives had begun to bend toward me when I neared them. Without stroking, they were all bending toward me. Knives bending, rings appearing. I stood looking out the window with Johnny Appleseed. I said I see it, Johnny. The trees are bleeding, the sap is flowing. He took out his knife. Stroke the blade, he said. Stroke the blade. It bent upward toward the sky. I see it bending, I said. I see it bending, they're all bending. More rings on my arm, a flat one around my waist. Two more flat ones which circled my breasts. A brass teakettle rocking on the stove like a blind singer. Johnny Appleseed went up to bed. I went to sleep in the garage.

I found a box in the garage, filled with toys, my artifacts. I lay on the mattress, surrounded by stuffed bears with music boxes, brass key wings plunged deep in their backs, rotating like hummingbirds. I caught a wing in my teeth, felt the metal cold and bitter on my tongue, let the notes out slowly. I held a bear to my chest, felt the humming of the song in the bear like a heartbeat. The bears stopped one by one. I continued holding on to them. I saw the door open; I'd known he would come. *Johnny Johnny Johnny Johnny whoops Johnny whoops Johnny.* He sat down cross-legged by the enameled lamp, the light modeling his face. Give me those, he said, it's the only way you'll live. I handed him the bears. He put them back in the box, pushed the box away, outside of where the light reached. He lay his hat over the lamp; it dimmed the light. He slipped off the apron. The shirt beneath was made without buttons and was open at the collar. He pulled it off over his head, the thick hair on his chest, the hair. He turned off the light then; the garage blackened. My blouse unbuttoning, jeans catching on rings. Hands moving up my belly, nipples rising as if by magic. Plant some, Johnny, plant. There is no garage, Johnny, I said. There is no house. No trees. No earth. Just this mattress, cool sheets, your voice in my ear. I can be in Zanzibar, Johnny, I said. I'm already there, I said. And I love it Johnny, it's nothing Johnny, it feels good Johnny Johnny, and empty Johnny, it's real Johnny Johnny, it's real Johnny, it's real.

The Clarence Roberts Mysteries

Michael Wilkerson

NASHVILLE—The body of a man was found Sunday in the remains of the fire-gutted home of Clarence and Geneva Roberts. Investigators believe the dead man was Roberts, but pathologists are still analyzing the evidence. It will be some time before a final determination can be made, police said.

Bloomington *Herald-Telephone,* Nov. 18, 1970

WE AROSE this morning to the radio playing all our old favorites. We scrambled the eggs to "Sergeant Pepper." We burnt the toast on "Imagine." The jockeys played tapes of "Happy Christmas" while we buckled our belts and donned our dresses. We can't make sense of this one, this additional death; we're still sorting out the Clarence Roberts thing, and Santa Claus is coming. John Lennon's dead. Rain's changing to snow, but we don't trust it.

We used to wait for Clarence Roberts to glide into Nashville, Indiana, peeling out by Moores' Fiesta, then a restaurant but now a liquor store, the same liquor store where Geneva Roberts, years later, bought her spirits. Moores' had a beguiling little neon nameplate, and Clarence, uniformed, stopped in for pie and coffee. He pointed his police interceptor V-8, a Dodge, toward the street, where vagrants cringed and criminals cowered. Clarence fueled himself then with sugar and caffeine, as we do now and did earlier this morning. Already we amend our beginning, fudging on the inexorable details of our lives, so very early in this-our-story.

141

The Brown County Coroner's Office today refused to issue a death certificate for Clarence Roberts. The body of Sunday's fire victim will be buried anonymously. The family, though, said it will hold funeral services for Clarence Roberts, as previously scheduled.

Clarence, when the caffeine hit, talked of massive sums, of leveraging, of limited partnerships and tax-incremental financing. All the money he had in the world came from his seven thousand a year as sheriff. It wasn't enough, even with the Dodge allowed for his personal use, in this our booming consumerist world, especially in Nashville, where, by the late 1960s, big money had ridden into town on its own inimitable motor scooter.

John Lennon had made his pepper and was looking into the possibilities behind the glass onion.

Clarence, tempted as we've described, promised himself investment pyramided on investment, starting with a little sure-fire apartment complex. Green carpets, steel sinks, movable walls. Then there'd be another loan, this time for a shopping center. Eventually, all that would be sold; he'd own the bank and give Geneva the biggest warmest house in all Indiana for Christmas, with fresh coffee and fresh apples—not better ones than Brown County's, but *different* ones, flown in each day from the Pacific Northwest. We think without hope of Harry and David, those magical fruitmongers in our magazines. They're dead now.

Two coroners disagree over identity of dead man

We'd remind Clarence that a rush was a rush, but that work was work, and that we couldn't talk any more about his crazy schemes, but that we had our (unstated) apprehensions. We'd leave him there, talking at the counter.

Insurance company denies million dollar payment to Geneva Roberts

And what kind of story do we have here? Where's the sense? We're beginning to worry, now that we have some facts, facts which are warm and true and brief, like breakfast: Clarence apparently did not perish in Fire Number One (1970, when the apartment complex had been repossessed and he was no longer sheriff), but Geneva and

Clarence both died Sunday, December 4, 1980, in a second, equally arsonistic fire. What, we wonder, had the old boy been up to all those years? Who was that poor fellow that got cooked the first time? Come to think of it, we're not so sure about that word "arson." So many questions the facts don't cover. Better roll up our sleeves and get to work.

Roberts seen in Mexico

The house would have gone up regardless: whoever did it needn't have used the gasoline, either time. What is the meaning of overkill? These Indiana hill houses are weather-riddled, paintless things. God knows we call them "rustic," but that's yet another word of oh so many that hide real thought. Poor Geneva shouldn't have had to bake pies for money to go to Moores' (once a restaurant but by then a liquor store), but these are *hard times* for the economy of this our country long may it wave, to say nothing of for us ourselves. Need we add that you and you and you and I, we've lost our spirit?

If not Clarence, then who?

O the melancholy that lurks in our headlines these brutal days. When the newspapers doubt themselves, can you and you and you and I be far behind? Tragedy lurks in indecision. We need elán. A foreign word. No wonder we need it. John Lennon, can you show us the way out of the dark murky hallway of our waffling?

A further problem: No one tolerates our charming rough edges anymore. You scratch my back and I scald yours. Whither trust? We still think Clarence did it, we'll always come back to that God knows, yes he does. Clarence did set both fires, most emphatically he did die twice, trying to make it cleaner and better the second time, for the clear and present benefit of the police, the courts, the experts, the certified, the non-certified, the storytellers on the Liar's Bench in downtown Nashville (built of stone to stop the flames), the filmmakers, the media analysts, the upstanding ordinary American taxpaying citizens of Brown County and surrounding areas (more on them later). We like a man who tries to get things right.

Yes, Clarence died not alone but for us, for you and you and you and I, for the current and former officials of Brown County, the chefs (head and assistant) of the Nashville House Restaurant—may they all talk in low tones of utmost respect as do we now. Yes, we believe, in our so very un-artificial hearts, that it was Clarence who fanned those flames, specifically for the representatives of the Dillinger Museum (where Geneva browsed on lunch breaks), and for all those of us who are determined to view these two inexplicable events as intellectual bookends of the decade 1970–1980 (may it rest for just a while in response to these fires, and this latest, numbing shooting; may it rest, this rain-changing-to-snow morning).

New leads

By the way, we've sampled that pie at the Nashville House, not knowing back then that Geneva made it. How our knowledge transforms the context, how much more *baked* that pie would have tasted! What we know now gives yet one more spice to those unwary apples. It's a taste we nearly recognize, one we labor to name.

More new leads

In a major book of that oh so malingering decade the 1970s, a well-known literary critic interrupts his own better judgment, takes us aside, grabs us by our buttonless shirt collars, and denounces every last bit of what we are doing here. Name your spice! What kind of story is this? he seems to be saying. He insists on a merry moral yes we will say it saccharine Christmas. He tells us to uplift and strengthen. Oh, what an impossible order! It is not that we are tired—we are downright frisky as a matter of fact—but we are urged not to make dark and paranoid connections between unrelated events, such as the two murders, arsons and the assassination of John Lennon, over which we uncontrollably grieve, unless we can resolve those connections in a way that would satisfy a few basic hungers of the spirit of man and/or woman as they/we live in this clumsy world today. Oh fiction critic, all we hunger for is some of that apple pie which, sadly, we can never have again. We don't want to tell who we are or why we're interested or what Clarence Roberts means. We're still there at the scene, pacing inside and outside the yellow plastic police line, helping the authorities scrape the ash off the rubble.

Roberts seen in Dallas

Well, we're back to 1968 again (the fall, but a little earlier this time of the page), and Clarence again is sheriff. Dead things just won't stay dead. Clarence books them and jails them. He stops them and howdies them. He dreams of untold profits. Magnanimously we allow him to choose between Nixon, Humphrey and Wallace while we chew mystified on a Brown County biscuit a la apple butter, the first of many such biscuits we will swallow in our tumultuous lives. We try to recall the French for "apple butter," but just at this very moment when we need so badly to sound educated, it slips from our grasp. We do not know much of what the candidates stand for nor do we believe what we hear, yet some of us vote anyway. We take our stands! We're getting exhausted, but we swim on, puzzled creatures in the freezing unpredictable stream that is life but that (ha, ha, fiction critic!) does not in our case here in Indiana follow that clean predictable course that leads to enlightenment. Sometimes, we say in our folksy disarming manner, we bite the fruit of knowledge only to choke horrifyingly on its very pit!

This would not apply to apples, we realize.

"I'm going back to the field," says Clarence, and what choice do we have but to follow, like those new mass-produced cameras that fix images forever in their rooms of darkness.

Court upholds insurance company; body not Roberts', judge rules

The countryside around Nashville is booming and decaying, of which more earlier. Clarence's people, the folks who came here in covered wagons when wagons had to be covered and coming was not such an easy thing as it is now with our police interceptor V-8's and our hilarious little putting Volkswagens, are aging peacelessly, desperately. Their sons and daughters have long left these glorious rattle-snaked hills, engaged in the same old stories of migration hope and disaster of which we nationally are so aware. The wind erodes the simple log cabins. The aluminum sides of mobile homes buckle under the sadness. We sons and daughters leave our parents behind, we choose to let them be, bereaved.

Roberts seen in Memphis

We remember the old Brown County stories, which explain how this village got its name, how that bear was slain shortly before it would have throttled the young Abe Lincoln, who visited here when times were different. He lit no fires. We can rest assured, along with our old nemesis, that big-time fiction critic. In this we are bedfellows.

Oooh, we say, such pretty hills! Is this what Abe Lincoln said? Did John Lennon speak similarly when he flew over this very spot on his way to the concert in Indianapolis lo so many years ago? Why, we'll sell our stock and move here! We'll build us a cedar shake cabin! As a matter of fact we have been busy doing just this and this and that, we have built how many cabins is it now honey we have filled the hills not to mention the dales they're there too and choice lots are still available, we have filled them with cabins we have built, and in so doing we have transmuted the meaning of the word "build," which in our case seems to mean "paid someone to build." Very well. We fill our days with trips to the Nashville House and Moores' Fiesta. We explore the Dillinger Museum in the wake of the theft of most of its contents, but soon the novelty fades. We grow increasingly introspective, turning ourselves inside out like shirts. We paint bad art and fob it off on tourists. We police the newspapers for clues. We send messages. Hello, Heidi. We fight property taxes. We refuse new schools. We are enraged. We are waiting still waiting for Clarence Roberts to come back home, to divert our minds from the mundane world we have built (see earlier reference). Christmas approaches us, feels our skin, singes our hair. We're just good country people, we're trying honestly to wrap things up, trying to get them neat, to cover their endlessness with scotch tape and foil bells. We've got holiday technology all over the house. Secretly we look forward to trashing the gift paper the moment it's been used; the colored stuff burns gorgeously under the hearth, we hear. We'll sweep it into the fireplace and see what happens.

Roberts seen in Bloomington

Well, hey, how about that, Clarence is at the house, the second of two (we hope it can be held to two, but we're getting increasingly nervous about anything that smacks of predictability). Geneva's out baking again, pocketing biscuits to bring to him whom the police can never seem to spot. Clarence has built himself a workshop in the old sense, and he's doing what a small-town sheriff does best—supervising himself. He uses his hands like an inmate. He's making nameplates. Taking names. We remember an old joke along those lines, but we can't piece together why it was funny. Still, we give ourselves over to laughter, but then remember that Clarence is a dangerous man, there in his workshop, etching a name—maybe that of John Lennon, George McGovern, Ronald Reagan, yours, ours. It's a simple process, really, an indentation and dyeing of plastic. Clarence will send poor Geneva around to talk to the neighbors, to hustle the plates. We buy ours and fasten it to the mailbox. Have we averted disaster? Jokingly we claim that we will buy yours and give it to you for Christmas (does this mean we're really Santa?) but no, oh no, we will never get the chance.

And what, furthermore, is Clarence thinking about us as he stands alone day after day, working oh so carefully on our names, the names our mothers most generally gave us? Is this what our fiction critic would call communication, this reaching out from a workshop we don't even know about? Speaking of the man himself, what would he tell us now? We fear we'll never know. We still don't know who set either of those fires, and clearly something very important is missing from our story. What a mystery. Aha, the thoughts of our protagonist, Clarence Roberts, are scarcely alluded to here! How can we tell his story when we don't know what he thinks? Our well-known critic might argue at this point that we have no story, since all stories have a plot and pattern that resolves itself in a way that uplifts and strengthens the moral fiber of we the readers. Tragically we must admit we just don't understand that kind of talk.

What we're really worried about are those damned nameplates.

Investigators reopen Roberts' case

Folly. We are backtracking and sidetracking here in the world of the editorial we. We hire intelligent dogs to sniff the remains of old Brown County in the overcast night. We're truly deregulated now, but we can't say why or wherein lies our principal interest, since we just can't find the killer(s). Problems, problems: our cute little Volkswagen won't start any more, our sleepwear is flammable, yet we continue to stumble, toward the true meaning of whatever we are seeking.

Towne Cinema burns; arson seen as possibility

Imagine a story of which we are reminded (previously told, we conscientiously credit) by Arthur C. Clarke, in which Tibetan monks hire a word processing consultant to expedite their eternal task, which is to transcribe each of the nine billion potential true names of God, one of which at this point better damned well be Clarence Roberts, and another we hope to be John Lennon. But what a story! We don't find out what we want to know. *We never see the list* (is Clarke withholding evidence that could have helped us solve this crime? Are these the Tibetan monks who build their temples in nearby Blooming-ton?). The story ends when the names are printed out dot-matrix style and the stars, like Clarence's apartment buildings, go plumb out of business. How many names did old Clarence take down in the ten years between the fires, anyway? We're nervous, so we look up; it's overcast. We won't know if we live until tomorrow. Another failed resolution.

Family disagrees over Roberts, breaks up

And so it is night, and the stars burn without mercy. We bury Clarence one more time. We dig out our funeral suits. (How they've shrunk! Has it really been ten years?) We hire an unsuspecting minister and an out-of-state poet to concoct a eulogy. We sit back and enjoy the show. Really big show, we can't help but think. What kind of story has this been? Sadly, we will never know. The inventory of the dead is tragically long. Our fiction critic, gone suddenly. John Lennon. Clar-ence. And Clarence. Clods fall on the impregnable vault, in which lie the worldly remains. When we breathe deeply, we can't deny the acrid smell, the sinister smoke.

Roberts house destroyed by fire; two bodies found

As if more flames could clear up the mystery. We are holding right here in our hands our soiled hands, yet another newspaper clipping, this one from New Jersey, of yet another arson-murder, of a corpse named Clarence Roberts, of a man seen fleeing. We hate coincidence! We won't give it the time of day. But here in our hands, we have this clipping, and as we hold it we know the cheap newsprint acid will consume it and we will be left with nothing, nothing but what we know is the God's truth.

Death goes on. The new President by now has appointed his cabinet and thus has ordered their nameplates. Look out. We fireproof the cedar shake of our cabin. S/he who killed Clarence Roberts is still on the loose, and we're without clues. Oh tragically mortal fiction critic, does that mean we were right all along? Tell us what you found in the rubble. We know in our hearts that all is not lost, that Santa Claus is coming to town, bringing more of his terrible gifts. Our lives are now declared officially out of hand. Someone sends us a fireplace set. There's much cringing in Brown County. Boots shake. We look at the angry black limbs of the trees, and it is nearing Christmas by cracky. In every chimney, there is too much soot.

Enjoy an old-time Brown County holiday this year!

We take the kids to the newly expanded shopping mall and wait in line to see the fat man. John Lennon's best songs have been transubstantiated. We listen to a sanitized "Give Peace a Chance" on the tinny speaker, and we have a pretty good idea who owns the Muzak business.

The lines to see Him are incredibly long. He's a chubby one, but let's face it, he could be anyone behind those whiskers and all that felt. Curious, those wire-rim glasses, that unforgettable chin. Note the hands. Those scars could be a platemaker's. The television reporters are here doing features, a man-in-the-street on John Lennon and the other about Santa himself, about the way you can rearrange all the letters in Santa and arrive at demonic new insights. How much irony can one story hold? Where oh where have we seen those reporters before? Ah. In Nashville. They've been there when we were there, checking the particulars, the foundation if you will, of the Roberts residence. They turn on their microphones and listen. Restless babies howl in the Mall. The President meets and meets and meets with his generals. Like all Presidents. He can't help it. It must be a disease, a virus in the White House, we shrewdly assert. We move to the front of the line, where we see tinsel, lights, holly, covering up everything. A clipboard and a pencil. A man looks dangerously at us and begins to write. Outside downtown, the roof implodes on the city's oldest remaining cinema. Flames extinguish the stars. A scarred man, sheriff-like, disappears in the confused crowd.

Grand Jury convenes again in Roberts case; aging coroner quits in huff

We blast way deep into the new decade. There will probably be many more unless the stars go out, but perhaps none like that last one. What a wild time that was! As we talk, grass covers the graves of all the Clarence Robertses in the known world. The Dillinger Museum diversifies into petty criminals. The out-of-state poet passes through and makes a note of it. He's far away, but he doesn't miss a thing. Old fads return. Hoola hoops and ankle sox. We play our records backwards, looking for clues. We learn more than we wanted to know. The poet says, it would have been good to grow old with John Lennon. Too bad, poet. Enough's enough. In the privacy of our homes, we weatherstrip the windows (how many years has it been?), bank the fires, turn down the TV news, and resurrect our lives.

Postcards

David Moser

1.

COUPLE no. 1, Brad and Janey, have just rounded the corner at Indiana Street and Kirkwood and are now headed west. They pass Mr. Zukav who has just left the Book Nook, under his arm a shoplifted paperback entitled *101 Things to Make with Human Skin,* which pretty well puts to rest the old adage that you can't judge a book by its cover. The stealthy Mr. Zukav goes unnoticed by couple no. 1, who, as usual, are deciding where to eat.

BRAD: Let's eat at The Gables, it's close by.
JANEY: You mean Garcia's?
BRAD: What did I say?
JANEY: You said The Gables. What's The Gables?
BRAD: Never mind. I meant Garcia's.
JANEY: We just passed by there.
BRAD: I know. Let's eat there.
JANEY: Okay, I just have to mail this postcard first.

They exit the scene. Mr. Zukav heads across the street, head buried in his book.

Couple no. 2, Rita and Marsha, have just attended a showing of the new Sylvester Stallone movie at the Von Lee. They emerge into the sunlight just in time to see Mr. Zukav, propelled by the bumper of an AMC jeep, flying through the air like Nijinsky. He lands head first at their feet with a thud and a hoarse exhalation of air.

RITA: As if we don't see enough violence at the movies, we have to see it in real life, too.
MARSHA: Yeah, really.

The ambulance arrives and almost runs over a careless bicyclist with a small harmonica-playing Colobus monkey perched on his shoulder. Soon the sidewalk is congested with pedestrians, police officers, squinting movie-goers exiting the theater, and pimply-faced video game players taking a break from zapping aliens to check out the excitement. One of the police officers on hand to dispel onlookers spies a young woman seated on a bench in People's Park breastfeeding twins.

COP: You'll have to do that somewhere else, lady.
MOTHER: You're kidding. I think I have a right to feed my babies whenever and wherever I see fit.
COP: Yeah, well it's indecent exposure.
MOTHER: To dirty minds like yours maybe. Go ahead and arrest me. All these people will be my witnesses.

The police officer gives up, turns away and pretends to help direct traffic away from the parked ambulance.
When he goes home that night he finds a postcard in his mailbox. On the glossy side is a trick photo of a rodeo cowboy seemingly riding a giant jackrabbit. The message on the back reads:

Mom—
My ears just popped and I can hear lots better now. For instance, there's a man in West Lafayette, Indiana, taking a piss while brushing his teeth. There's a couple shouting at each other in heavily-accented English somewhere in West Africa, and someone just dropped a fork in the middle of the word "nuclear" at a restaurant in the United

Nations Building. Lots of sibilant, clangy sounds out there. I'll keep you informed.

Your son,
Brad

This isn't for me, the police officer thinks.

2.

The nurse is filling out Mr. Zukav's hospital medical record. She estimates his weight, checks the color of his hair and eyes and briefly summarizes the circumstances of his admission to the hospital: Elderly white male, struck by motor vehicle while on foot. Broken bones, lacerations, some internal bleeding and injuries, may require surgery, etc. etc. She comes to a section of the form which reads "Patient's mental state upon admission:

Alert ☐ Confused ☐ Unconscious ☐ ." She checks "Confused."

NURSE: Mr. Zukav, Doctor Smith will be here soon to look at you. But in the meantime we might as well get as much information from you as we can. Will that be okay? First of all, are you married?

ZUKAV: Not any more.

NURSE: What is your occupation?

ZUKAV: I make plastic swords.

NURSE: Pardon?

ZUKAV: I work for Webster, Inc. They make toys. I make toy plastic swords for them. We've been in business since the fifties making the same plastic sword. Only the packaging changes. When I started out it was called the Erroll Flynn Pirate Sword, then the Three Musketeers Sabre. In the early sixties we called it the Genuine Mark of Zorro Cutlass, and then we changed it to the Luke Skywalker Laser-Light Sword when the crazy Star Wars thing came along. Right now we're calling it the Rambo "First Blood" Machete. We do a steady business.

The nurse rapidly pens a concise approximation of his reply in the space marked "Occupation." She is young, aloof, efficient. Despite his pain, Mr. Zukav finds himself wanting to touch her leg, a beautiful Platonic thing half-covered in hospital white, just out of his reach.

3.

Couple no. 3, Stan and Patty, are checking out of room 306 at the Holiday Inn on Highway 37 on the way to Indianapolis. They have paid $50 for an evening of uninterrupted privacy. Stan shares a small apartment with a studious, stay-at-home linguistics major, and Patty lives at home with her parents. As Stan returns the room key to the front desk he overhears a conversation between the motel clerk and a long-haired musician.

MOTEL CLERK: May I help you?

BAND MEMBER: Yes, I'm with a group called UFO, which stands for "United Funk Organization." We travel all over the Midwest playing gigs, which is a hard life these days because there are so few clubs that hire live bands anymore, you know. So if you don't mind, the band is pretty tired and we'd like to go to our rooms as soon as possible. That is to say, these six exhausted Negroes and one somewhat less exhausted white boy who has been chosen as a spokesperson for the group, that is, most motel night clerks being white, yourself being no exception, that is, our music being as funky and danceable as it is, we find ourselves expending a great deal of energy and what we would like now is to go to our rooms so that we might crash and smoke the rest of the dope hidden in the inner recesses of our keyboard player's Hammond B-3 organ, and what I'd like to know is, do we all have to register separately or can I just sign for all of us?

After dropping Patty off at her place Stan returns home to find a postcard in his mailbox. On the front is a photo of some university students in front of the Musical Arts Center staring up at an Alexander Calder sculpture as if it were a landed alien spaceship. On the back of the postcard is printed:

Dear Stan,
    If I should become famous years from now, would you tell people about the big birthmark on my right breast that looks like an

extra nipple, and about how I have to sleep with the radio on all night? Well if you do, so help me I'll go on nationwide TV and tell everyone how you got drunk one night and wet the bed, and how your cocker spaniel died because you went off for a month and forgot to get someone to feed it, and how you were impotent with me for a whole year. I'm not famous yet, but just keep it in mind. Honesty is the best policy, right?

> Sincerely,
> Rita

Stan crumples the postcard in his hand. *Jeez,* he thinks, *the woman who still hides her birth control pills when her mother comes to visit is telling* me *about honesty.*

4.

Couple no. 2, Rita and Marsha, have stopped at the corner of Sixth and Dunn to observe the impossibly small monkey perched on the shoulder of a Woodstock generation bicyclist. The monkey is playing "The Yellow Rose of Texas" on the harmonica as the bicyclist chomps into a sandwich he just bought at the Bloomingfoods Co-op. Strands of alfalfa sprouts cling to his beard, indistinguishable from the gray hairs.

RITA: That monkey is incredibly far-out. Where did you get it?
BICYCLIST: Some new place in Dunnkirk Square called Primate Heaven.
RITA: Yeah, every time you turn around there's a new shop there.
MARSHA: Can he play any other songs?
BICYCLIST: Sure. He's a very eclectic performer.
RITA: Can he play the Mozart piano concerto in D minor, K. 466?
BICYCLIST: Only the exposition.
MARSHA: Can he improvise?
BICYCLIST: Don't be ridiculous.

Rita and Marsha depart, enthusiastically headed for Primate Heaven. The bicyclist goes home to water his plants. Upon inspecting his mailbox he discovers a world-weary postcard with a faded photo of Elvis Presley on the front. The King of Rock and Roll is posed next to the ruins of the Acropolis, guitar in hand and smiling his crooked, sexy smile. On the back of the card, in pencil, is scrawled:

> Dear Lisa,
>   Having a wonderful time here in Athens. Saw the new Woody Allen movie with subtitles in Greek. Really interesting! I don't think the audience understood it. Ate some weird food yesterday and threw up. I miss you constantly and think about you all the time. I haven't yet figured out why I'm here. Can I come home soon?
>
> Love,
Mark

This isn't for me, the bicyclist thinks.

5.

The police officer has just finished a Swanson's TV dinner: Salisbury steak with brown onion gravy, hashed brown potato nuggets, peas and carrots in seasoned sauce, and apple cake cobbler for dessert. Now he is watching a popular nighttime game show.

MODERATOR: . . . our ten-point bonus question. Girls, which horror movie title will your husband say best describes your honeymoon night: *Invasion of the Body Snatchers, Jaws,* or *Night of the Living Dead?* Sheila, which do you think Bob will choose?
SHEILA: I'd have to say . . . uh . . . could you read those again?

The police officer picks up his loaded revolver and points it at the embarrassed young contestant on the screen who seems totally unaware of his actions. His face betraying no emotion, the police officer whispers:
Bang.
Bang.
Bang.
It is not the first time he has done this.

6.

The future is inevitable. Stan, headed toward the Student Union, is aware that soon he will have to walk in front of Max, legendary campus evangelist, self-appointed bringer of the Gospel to a godless and sneering crowd of college students near Ballantine Hall. Stan decides to sit down on the grass near the circle of spectators to watch. Max, tattered Bible in hand, is just now reaching the climax of his open-air impromptu sermon, his face becoming as red as watermelon at the county fair.

MAX: IT'S NOT EASY TO WALK IN THE PATH OF RIGHTEOUSNESS ON THIS WICKED CAMPUS. SOME OF YOU DON'T SEEM TO CARE. DO YOU HAVE ANY IDEA HOW MANY YOUNG WOMEN WHO COME HERE TURN INTO HARLOTS AND WHORES?

MALE HECKLER: Phone numbers, Max! Phone numbers!

Stan becomes distracted by the bemused coed sitting next to him on the grass. His eyes scan the slope of her forehead, her long, brown hair, the curve of her back. She seems relaxed, totally at ease. He glances at the titles of the books on the ground next to her: *The Tao of Physics* and *A Sanscrit Word Count in Joyce's Finnegans Wake*. Just my type, Stan thinks. He finds himself wishing to make contact with her, to share his innermost thoughts with fearless and unashamed immediacy. He wants to say "We are kindred spirits, you and I, both students of the fascination and folly of humankind." He also wants to touch her neck. Instead he watches as she rises to greet her boyfriend with a breezy kiss.

7.

Dr. Smith leaves the hospital a little earlier than usual, since the only interesting case to come his way all day was some codger who had gotten himself run over crossing the street on Kirkwood. Tonight is Dr. Smith's 25th wedding anniversary and they've invited some guests over for dinner. His wife has prepared an elaborate meal.

The knife feels familiar in the doctor's hand. It is for him a temperature more than anything else, a steely coldness which cooperatively remains rigid in his hand as he prepares to carve the turkey. In contrast to the hot meat, steaming gravy, warm rolls, and tepid conversation, the metal is refreshingly cool. The knife seems to him a patriarchal scepter, a utensil of stately midwestern utilitarianism. It is the frontier link, the crucial node between his own lofty moral sense and the somewhat grittier what-must-be-done-dammit. The philosophy of the knife, like that of the scalpel, is alteration, dissolution, the splitting up of objects into their component parts. And so the anonymous bird submits to its destiny, 20-plus pounds about to be dissipated to constituent chemicals through the bodies and bowels of these smiling guests. The first incision obscures the metallic reflection of empty plates and smiling faces on the blade. Dr. Smith's hand trembles slightly as he encounters opposition, but the knife remains dependably solid. It is a still a mystery to him why the everyday objects he holds in his hands don't fly apart in a spray of quarks.

The bird now opened in front of him, Dr. Smith prepares to scoop out some of what is inside for his guests, but suddenly notices something amiss.

Honey, what is a postcard doing stuffed inside the turkey?

8.

Marsha is seated in the Commons at the Student Union eavesdropping on a conversation between three women at the table next to her.

FIRST WOMAN: . . . and it suddenly dawned on me one day that my relationship with this woman had become just as tedious as being with a man . . .

SECOND WOMAN: I just wanna get out of here so bad, you know? This town . . . what can I say? If I didn't have . . . if I weren't so close to finishing . . .

THIRD WOMAN: . . . and I thought, as well him as another, and so, yes, I said, yes . . .

How long can a conversation continue with no one paying any attention to what the others are saying? wonders Marsha. The jukebox begins to play "Heard It Through the Grapevine" for the third time in an hour. Marsha stands to leave and there is a blood-curdling scream from the bowling alley. Gutter ball, she thinks. She stops for a second on the way to the women's room to check her watch and is brusquely rotated 90 degrees in her tracks by an enormous bass fiddle. She looks up to see a jazzer from the School of Music hurrying to a jam session. Oblivious to the fact that he has just rammed her with his instrument, he is singing a Gershwin tune out loud:

> *Although I can't dismiss*
> *The memory of her kiss . . .*

Marsha considers following him for a little while but thinks better of it.

9.

Janey is at the kitchen sink preparing dinner. Her hands bear the minute evidences of past kitchen mishaps, little pink hyphens on the thumb and index finger where the knife sliced human being instead of carrot. The TV is on, and she is watching an impossibly old rerun of *I Love Lucy*. The thought occurs to her: Will my marriage to Brad be as durable as these old TV shows? She is remembering the day before the wedding when the minister met with them in his office. He served them white wine. There was a photo of Fritz Perls hanging above the bookshelf.

"Keep the relationship alive, exciting," he had advised them. "Don't fall into ruts. If one of you wants to do it doggie style, do it doggie style."

Doggie style.

He was a Unitarian minister, of course.

She is remembering the unexpected sinking feeling which accompanied the vows. She sees her hands, the way they trembled when Brad placed the ring on her finger. Why had they trembled? Not from nervousness exactly. Something other than nervousness. This isn't for me, she had thought at the time.

The minister's voice sounded triumphant as he read the line which had been included at the request of Brad's mother: "What God has joined, let no man put asunder."

Asunder.

10.

Marsha is mystified by the postcard she has just discovered lying on the street. There is no return address, and it is simply addressed to "My Friends." She reads the message printed in purple felt-tip pen:

Hi—

In *The Brain from Planet Arous* the alien brain occupied, among other things, a helpless dog. The dog's consciousness, at this point being crowded out of its host, no doubt felt compelled to occupy something else, perhaps my Swanson's TV dinner. This explains a great deal, I think. In *Attack of the Crab Monsters* the alien being was housed inside giant crabs. Which is a very different situation, of course.

Love,
A Police Officer

Marsha's puzzled thoughts are interrupted by a young long-haired musician carrying a trumpet case.

"Excuse me, miss, I'm here with my friends, we're with a band called UFO. We play a mixture of funk and rock and cover tunes from the sixties and seventies, and we travel a lot playing gigs around the Midwest and, well, we frankly get a bit lonely sometimes, being on the road and all, and we find ourselves here in your town for a day or two playing at the Bluebird, and not knowing anyone, being total strangers and all, well, we were just wondering if you could tell us—where do they keep all the black women in this town?"

11.

Couple no. 1, Brad and Janey, are headed south on Dunn Street discussing the relative merits of New York City vs. Bloomington. Couple no. 2, Rita and Marsha, are walking east on Kirkwood lamenting the unexpected rise of the religious right. Couple no. 3, Stan and Patty, have just exited Kilroy's, slightly drunk, uninhibitedly discussing, among other things, the possibility of communication with extraterrestrial beings.

At precisely 8:03 p.m. all three couples inadvertently collide at the corner of Kirkwood and Dunn.

BRAD: Oops, sorry there . . .

PATTY: . . . I mean, how would you even *know* there was a message there, right? It could just be gibberish . . .

MARSHA: Sorry, I didn't see you folks . . .

JANEY: . . . You can just think of this as your home base or something, and make as many trips to the east coast as you want . . . Oh, sorry . . .

STAN: . . . so what are the aliens gonna think when they get this Chuck Berry record and they have to figure out, you know, is this Earth music or what? . . .

RITA: Whoops, 'scuse me!

BRAD: . . . Yeah, but not just *any* small town. It would have to be a university town like this one where you have all this, you know, culture or whatever . . .

MARSHA: . . . To me it's real creepy, you know, you see these people in McDonald's bowing their heads to pray before they eat their Big Mac . . .

PATTY: So you'd have to explain it and then explain the explanation and then explain the explanation of the explanation . . .

STAN: Sorry, we didn't see you coming . . .

RITA: . . . and any minute the guy who's helping you try on your shoes might whip out his Bible or something and start witnessing, and there you are, you can't run away . . .

BRAD: . . . but really, everything you *really* need is right here, right here, right here . . .

In the midst of the confusion Stan is nearly poked in the eye by a small boy wielding a Rambo "First Blood" plastic machete.

"Watch it, punk," he says, shoving the child against a wall.

Patty turns to Marsha. "Stan has been a real jerk since he got his self-esteem back," she says, patting the little waif on the head. The boy clutches his toy sword to his chest, protecting his wounded pride as he watches the couples regroup and stroll their separate ways, Brad with Marsha, Janey with Stan, Rita with Patty.

12.

The nurse checks Mr. Zukav's vital signs, fluffs his pillow, presents him with his morning mail: perfunctory get-well cards from his boss and his ex-wife, and a postcard with no return address. Mr. Zukav puts on his bifocals and reads the printed message with trembling hands:

> Dear Friends,
>   There is a malevolent and oppressive force at work here causing us to repeat trite and nonproductive themes over and over again. You may safely ignore most of our art, music, literature, and cinema, as there is little likelihood that you will find anything worthwhile there.
>   Sincerely,
>   The Creative Forces in America

This isn't for me, Mr. Zukav tells the nurse as he slips into unconsciousness.

ACKNOWLEDGMENTS

"Everybody Watching and the Time Passing Like That," copyright © by Michael Martone. First published in *Alive and Dead in Indiana* (Alfred A. Knopf, 1984). Appeared previously in *Fort Wayne Is Seventh on Hitler's List* (Indiana University Press, 1990). Reprinted by permission of the author.

"A History of Indiana," copyright © by Jesse Lee Kercheval. First published in *The Dogeater* (University of Missouri Press, 1987). Reprinted by permission of the author.

"The First Journey of Jason Moss," copyright © by Scott Russell Sanders. First published in *Poet & Critic,* vol. 16, no. 2, 1985. Reprinted by permission of the author.

"I Can If I May," copyright © by James Alexander Thom. Excerpted from the novel *Staying Out of Hell* (Ballantine Books, 1985). Reprinted by permission of the author.

"The Night Coach to Bloomington," copyright © by Lee Zacharias. Excerpted from the novel *Lessons* (Houghton Mifflin, 1981). Reprinted by permission of the William Morris Agency, Inc. on behalf of the author.

"Can I Just Sit Here for a While?" copyright © by Ron Hansen. First published in *Atlantic Monthly,* December 1978. Appeared previously in *Matters of Life and Death* (Wampeter Press, 1983) and *Nebraska* (Atlantic Monthly Press, 1989). Reprinted by permission of Atlantic Monthly Press and the author.

"Blessing," copyright © by Elizabeth Stuckey-French. First published under the title "Mixed Blessings" in *Indiannual 4,* 1988. Reprinted by permission of the author.

"The First Winter of My Married Life," copyright © by William H. Gass. First published by Lord John Press, 1979. Reprinted by permission of the author.

"Johnny Appleseed," copyright © by Susan Neville. First published in *Apalachee Quarterly,* 1978. Appeared previously in *Pushcart Prize IV* (Avon, 1979) and in *The Invention of Flight* (University of Georgia Press, 1984). Reprinted by permission of the author.

"The Clarence Roberts Mysteries," copyright © by Michael Wilkerson. First published under the title "The Clarence Roberts' Mystery Story" in *Indiana Review,* vol. 8, no. 1, 1985. Reprinted by permission of the author.

"Postcards," copyright © by David Moser. First published in *The Ryder,* vol. 1, no. 31, 1980. Reprinted by permission of the author.

163

DEBORAH GALYAN, co-editor of *New Territory,* is a graduate of The Johns Hopkins University Writing Seminars. Her fiction has appeared in *The North American Review, Chicago Review,* and in a variety of newspapers. She has won a PEN Syndicated Fiction Prize and a Wisconsin Arts Board Fellowship. She is a former fiction editor of *Indiana Review.* She lives with her husband, Michael Wilkerson, in Lake Forest, Illinois, where she is currently at work on a collection of short fiction.

WILLIAM H. GASS is the author of the novel *Omensetter's Luck,* the short story collection *In the Heart of the Heart of the Country,* and several volumes of criticism and philosophy, including *The World within the Word* and *On Being Blue.* He taught philosophy at Purdue University in the 1960s and currently teaches at Washington University in St. Louis.

RON HANSEN was born in Nebraska and was educated at Creighton University, the University of Iowa's Writers' Workshop, and Stanford University, where he held a Wallace Stegner Creative Writing Fellowship. He is the author of two novels, *Desperadoes* and *The Assassination of Jesse James by the Coward Robert Ford,* as well as a children's book, *The Shadow Walker,* and a collection of short stories, *Nebraska.* In 1970 he was stationed at Fort Benjamin Harrison in Indianapolis.

JESSE LEE KERCHEVAL teaches at the University of Wisconsin-Madison. She has also taught at DePauw University in Greencastle. Her short story collection, *The Dogeater,* won the 1987 Associated Writing Programs Award in Short Fiction and was published by the University of Missouri Press.

MICHAEL MARTONE grew up in Fort Wayne. He is the author of two collections of stories, *Alive and Dead in Indiana* and *Safety Patrol.* He recently edited *A Place of Sense, Essays in Search of the Midwest* and is currently working on a series of personal essays about the Midwest. He is a Briggs-Copeland lecturer in fiction at Harvard University and lives with his wife, Theresa Pappas, and his son, Sam.

DAVID MOSER's master's degree in music was begun at Indiana University-Bloomington in 1979, but after a complex period of transformation, it somehow metamorphosed into a master's degree in Chinese at the University of Michigan in 1989. Currently, he is back in Bloomington doing China-related activities and working as a research assistant in cognitive science. His fiction has appeared in Indiana journals such as *Indiana Review, Quarry, The Ryder,* and *Streets,* as well as in *Mississippi Review* and *Scientific American.*

SUSAN NEVILLE's collection of stories *The Invention of Flight* won the Flannery O'Connor Award for Short Fiction and was published by the University of Georgia Press. She was born in Indianapolis and has lived in Henry and Putnam counties. She is currently an associate professor of English at Butler University in Indianapolis.

SCOTT RUSSELL SANDERS is connected to Indiana through his feet, most of the time, because he lives there and has lived there since 1971, teaching at Indiana University-Bloomington. He has published twelve books, including *Wilderness Plots, Stone Country, The Paradise of Bombs,* and *The Invisible Company.* He recently completed a new collection of essays, *Secrets of the Universe.* He is at work on three new projects—a collection of stories, a novel about the history of the universe, and a study of the lives of physicists. He shares his house with his wife and two children.

ELIZABETH STUCKEY-FRENCH grew up in Lafayette and graduated from Purdue in 1980. After five years as a social worker in Virginia, she returned to Indiana and received a Master's Degree in creative writing from Purdue in 1989. She was awarded a fellowship from the Indiana Arts Commission in 1988. Her stories have appeared in *Prairie Winds, Indiannual 4,* and *Arts Indiana.* She lives with her husband in rural Tippecanoe County.

JAMES ALEXANDER THOM, a native of Owen County who now lives in rural Monroe County, is the author of several best-selling novels, including *Panther in the Sky, Follow the River,* and *Long Knife.* Before becoming a full-time fiction writer, he was a journalist for the *Indianapolis Star* and the *Fort Lauderdale News* and an editor of the *Saturday Evening Post.*

MICHAEL WILKERSON, co-editor of *New Territory,* has published stories and essays in *TriQuarterly, The Iowa Review, Negative Capability,* and *Where We Live: Essays about Indiana.* He was the founding editor of the *Indiana Review* and taught at the University of Wisconsin-Madison. He is currently the director of Ragdale Foundation, a retreat for artists, writers, and composers, in Lake Forest, Illinois.

LEE ZACHARIAS, a native of Chicago, is the author of the novel *Lessons* and the short story collection *Helping Muriel Make It through the Night.* She directs the Master of Fine Arts Program in Creative Writing and edits the *Greensboro Review* at the University of North Carolina-Greensboro.